AF241683

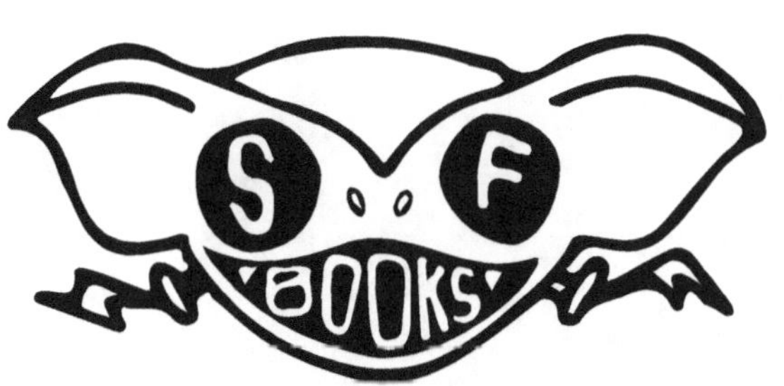

S F
BOOKS

SPARK & FIZZ BOOKS PRESENTS

PLANET SCUMM

SPRING 2020   "SIDEWAYS INFINITY"   ISSUE NO. 8

—— A FINITE TABLE OF CONTENTS ——

EDITOR IN CHIEF	CREATIVE DIRECTOR	MANAGING EDITOR	EDITOR	EDITOR
SEAN CLANCY	*ALYSSA ALARCÓN SANTO*	*TYLER BERD*	*ERIC LOUCKS*	*SAM RHEAUME*

COVER BY JORDAN ALARCON | *@JORDANALARCON*   **SPOT ART BY SAM RHEAUME** | *SAMRHEAUME.COM*

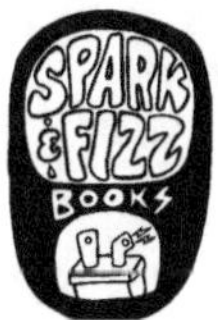

Planet Scumm is a triannual short fiction anthology. Visit **planetscumm.space** for submissions.

© SPARK & FIZZ BOOKS

First Printing, 2020   ISBN: 978-1-970154-05-4   *Portland | Boston | New York*

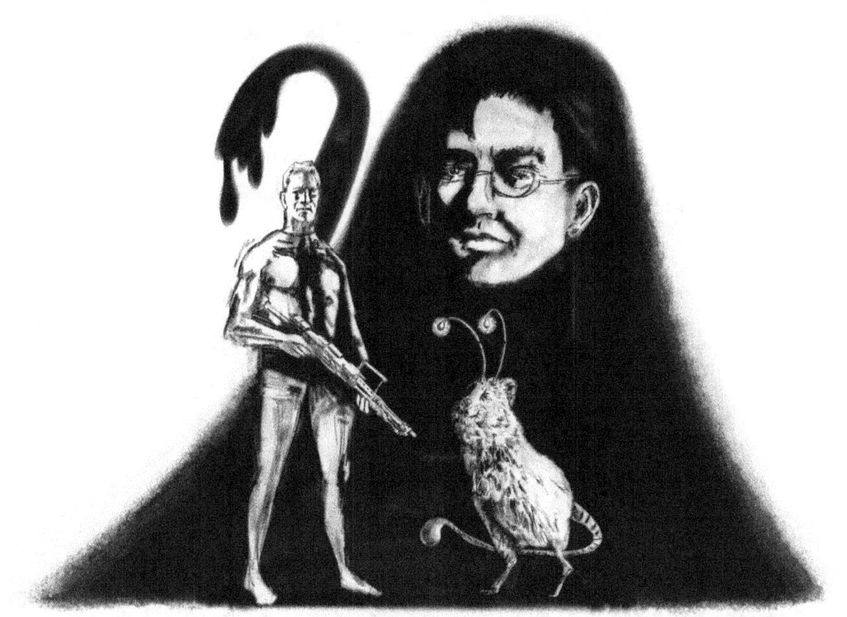

MISSION: SCUMM

So... you did it? You killed Scummy. Snuck aboard that floating circus he calls "Planet Scumm"? Vaporized him at point-blank range? Got revenge for the near-destruction of Earth? You did. Did all of that. Well... Super, then.

Disappointed? No, no it's not that, exactly. It's just that we were having fun being "shadowy contractors of bounty hunters." There was like a twenty year period, MAX, where that was even a thing on Earth. Plus we Earthers— humans, I mean—are new to the galaxy, and we were getting some pretty crazy sympathy donations.

I guess part of me wishes you'd been handily defeated. You know, as sort of a warning to us that Scummy wasn't to be trifled with. Then we'd contract out to another merc who'd fail, then another, until eventually settling for a bunch of burn-outs who are the only ones stupid enough to take the bounty.

But you got him in one. More's the pity. Here's your weird space money. See you around!

💾

Blasted Earthers. Scummy did the universe a favor by trashing that stupid continent of theirs. Two continents? Whatever, Z3B. Send over the new bounties. Gotta take my mind off this last job.

All right, let's take a look... Got something flagged here by Maya Dworsky-Rocha, codename *"Bookends."* Huh, looks like there's a dying planet out there that's using people as a form of living record-keeping, sharing memories and experiences and such, so that they never forget their homeworld. Sounds...touching. Absolutely, soul-achingly touching, and WAY too messy for bounty work. Let's keep looking.

Hey, remember Harris Coverley? The guy from the thing at the place? He sent us a sweet tip. Like, *actually*—he calls it *"A Taste of the Sweet Stuff."* This one has everything. Scientists, remote research station, government money—it's perfect. Might have to deal with a couple hundred thousand robotic bees, but hey, that's why we got in this business, right? Hmm? Well, it's why *I* got in this business. Partially. For the bees.

Hmm... Not an official request, but Steve DuBois has a profile tagged *"Prodigal"* making the rounds. Some religious group has set-up a low-tech colony on a nearby planet. Sounds like the kind of place a juicy target might flee to if they wanted to avoid detection, eh? Worst-case scenario: we don't find anybody worth shooting, but still walk away with some hand-woven baskets. Bounties *never* expect the ol' "wicker grenade."

Think we're ready to go after another morpher? Maureen Bowden's got a whole file here on *"Shapeshifters."* These ones don't sound too bad—birds, snakes, couple wolves. But it feels like that's what we *always* say when we go after morphers. "This will be easy! It's only a chipmunk!" Then the little bastard pulls a neutron pulser out of those chubby little cheeks and- well, you know how that one went. You don't? Well, there's a reason you're Z3B, not Z2B—let's just leave it at that.

We're skipping this corrections job, too. I heard all I needed to about that planet's prison system from Anna Catalano. They stick convicts in cramped isolation booths, and force them to solve puzzles and eat nutrient cubes for the duration. I forget the name of the program... *"Lazarus,"* or something like that. Total cranial disintegration is one thing, but *Sudoku*? I'd never let them take me alive.

Oooh, now this *is* interesting, Z3B. Company's getting notes from Luke Foster, our "theoretical biologics" consultant, that there's some sort of "extra-

MISSION: SCUMM

temporal" being causing havoc in some colonized areas. Time displacement... appears and disappears seemingly at-will...territoriality and a tendency towards attachment—this has "us" all over it! Lemme just get my- wait. A *DOG?* We can't kill a *"Good Boy"*! Forget it. We pull this job and we'll have a bigger bounty on our heads than Scummy ever did.

Hold on, Z3B, why the long face? And by "long face" I mean "Why are you projecting the 'crying emoji' from your eye sensors?" Do I feel conflicted about the Scummy bounty? Why should I be? See, I know something those Earthers don't. Something I found and neglected to mention at the payoff. See, this isn't the first time Scummy's been "terminated." Not by a longshot...

PLANET SCUMM ISSUE #8

SIDEWAYS INFINITY

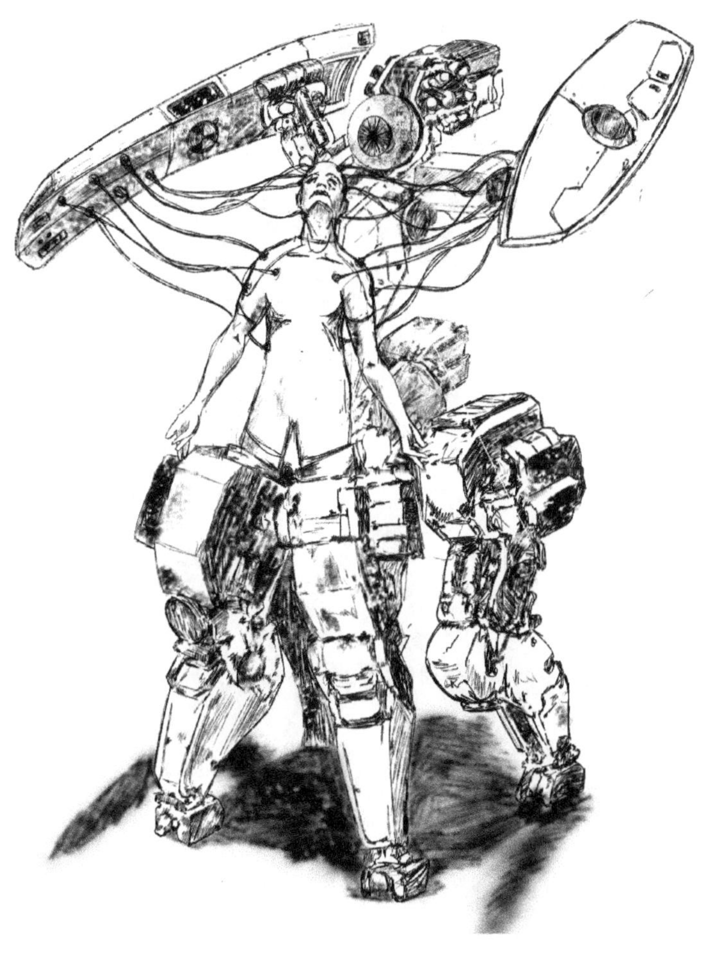

Spark & Fizz Books, 2020
Portland | Boston | New York

AUTHOR BIOS

MAYA DWORSKY-ROCHA is a doctoral candidate at Brandeis University, and a Fellow at the Schusterman Center for Israel Studies. She studies childhood and pedagogy, and is currently conducting fieldwork in Israeli educational institutions. Like most anthropologists, Maya has always been fascinated by science fiction's role as the vanguard of transformational thought. Maya lives with her wife in Boston MA, where she spends her time reading Terry Pratchett and Ursula Le Guin, and writing the kind of novels she wished had existed when she was growing up.

HARRIS COVERLEY lives in Manchester, England, where he awaits transcendence (or at least a new job opportunity). He had the idea for "A Taste of the Sweet Stuff" at the age of 15, and, unfortunately, since then the overall situation has grown worse. In addition to *Planet Scumm*, Harris also has short fiction published or forthcoming in *Curiosities*, *The J.J. Outré Review*, and *The Sirens Call*. He is also a member of the Weird Poets Society, and has had poetry most recently published in *Star*Line*, *Jitter*, and *Bewildering Stories*.

STEVE DuBOIS is a high school teacher from Kansas City. He has been shortlisted for the James White and Baen Fantasy Adventure Awards, and is the author of numerous works of speculative fiction and drama. His author site is stevedubois.net.

MAUREEN BOWDEN is a Liverpudlian living with her musician husband in North Wales. She has had 118 stories and poems accepted by paying markets and was nominated for the 2015 international Pushcart Prize. *Alban Lake* recently published *Whispers of Magic*, an anthology of her stories. Maureen also writes song lyrics, mainly comic political satire.

ANNA CATALANO's first short story, "Cry Sanctuary," was published in *Luna Station Quarterly Magazine*, and her story "Old Ink" is in an upcoming issue of Peculiar Journal. Catalano is half of a co-writing duo signed to publish their debut novel under the joint pen name Sylvia Barry. In 2018, Catalano traveled to Portugal for DISQUIET's annual writing workshop. She recently lived in Israel while finishing a novel, and hopes to do more traveling in the future.

LUKE FOSTER is a writer from Charlotte, NC. He writes everything from comedy to horror, and his stories have been published in both the US and UK. Recent stories include "Code Gray" for *Kzine Magazine*, "Bedbug" in *Jitter Press*, and "Blackout" for *Crimson Streets*. He has self-published comics since 2008. Recent releases include comedy/horror anthology "Spookytown" and the all-ages action-comedy "Doctor Bananas: Monkey Magician." Luke can be found online, usually on Twitter, at @ImLukeFoster.

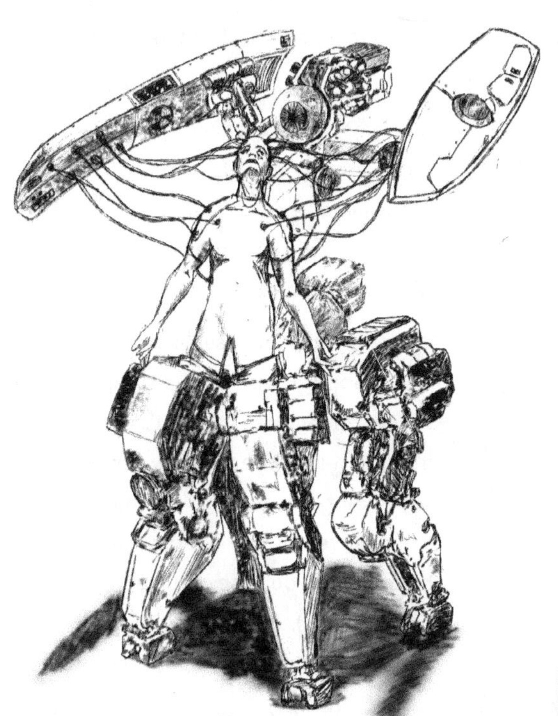

MAYA DWORSKY-ROCHA

BOOKENDS

Jenny's heart was beating so fast she could feel it in her teeth like a fun, crunchy buzz. Her nose felt like it could fly. That was a weird feeling to have in her nose, aerodynamic nostrils tensing as she plunged back into the water. Bubbles streamed past her eyebrows, and her hands hit the rough concrete of the poolside just as the whistle—

Jenny Winslow won the 100-meter in Beederman County's Annual Junior Aquatic Meet. Her time was one minute and twelve seconds. That wasn't her best time, though—her *best* was a minute flat, but it had only happened once (and, maybe, the timer hadn't been pressed at just the right moment).

Jenny was happy with her time. Her hair felt tight and her chest hurt and her teeth were still buzzing, but she was happy. The last kid who'd won this was almost thirteen, and Jenny was only eleven since April, so there.

The crowd cheered, and Mom and Coach bundled Jenny into a towel and brought her to the car. They got her cheap, chemical-tasting vanilla ice cream on the way home. It was her favorite and she could feel the fakeness travel down into her body and up her face, settling heavy and smooth in her eyebrows. Jenny was happy and tired and full of yummy chemicals. Jenny was falling asleep. Jenny was—

💾

The suit powers down and I steel myself for the pain of disconnect.

Archivist Marigold-Jay-359, reidentify.

I force my lips apart. They sting, but I manage. "Zophiella Raqib." I lick my lips and the skin is sharp and crumbly and bitter. I miss Jenny's ice cream.

Archivist Marigold-Jay-359, present three personal characteristics.

The suit sits me up, slowly making room between itself and my skin. I can move my fingers and toes. "I'm eleven and a half years old. My favorite color is blue, but not a dark blue. I like drawing."

Your three are accepted.
Have a good night's rest, Zophi.

I step out of the suit, and my arms and legs are still buzzing from Jenny's race. Not really, obviously, otherwise my biceps would be shiny and taut like hers instead of gray and skinny, with flappy skin. Momma keeps reminding me that what Jenny does only happens in my brain. That means it's important to move even if I'm tired from her swim meet, and eat even if I can still taste her ice cream.

Samantha, Momma's Book, has diabetes, and Momma says she feels guilty eating sweets even when she's outtasuit. She says "Sam's got diabetes, not Dina. I'm Dina, not Sam." Dina's my Momma's name.

When I'm outtasuit I just feel tired. And floppy. I wish I was sleeping, like Jenny. The Scribes say that's natural and it'll get better when I grow up; Momma says you get used to it. It's important to spend a few hours outtasuit every day because if you lose yourself, you're a bad Archivist. Archivists who get lost get pulled from their Books and retired.

"Zophi my love, eat." Momma pushes more pickles my way, and I munch obediently.

The canteen fluorescents make my eyeballs hurt. "Jenny won her swim meet."

"That's cool. Sam's houseplants are dying and it's *weighing* on her." Momma rolls her eyes and reaches for more Jalebi. When she's annoyed with Sam, Momma eats more sweets, and syrupy crunchiness is her favorite.

I don't usually get annoyed with Jenny. I like Jenny, and when she gets annoyed with herself I usually just feel bad. Momma says that, as we get older, Jenny will get on my nerves, just I wait.

Sarathiel comes by to collect our plates, and Momma gives her a kiss upside the head. Sarathiel smiles at me and I smile back because Momma's embarrassing even to kids who aren't *her* kids.

"You okay, Sarathi?" Momma's holding onto Sarathiel, but gently. "You dreaming?"

"Just started to." Sarathiel is two years older than me but her voice is soft and shy.

"It feels like being insuit when your Book's sleepy or sick." She leans into Momma and sighs, "It's not that different than Kate was towards the end."

Sarathiel's Book died. It's really bad when that happens. Now she's stuck: too old to take on a new Book, but too young to take on one of the old ones whose Archivist has died. Archivists and Books are meant to be as close in age as possible, so when one of them dies it throws everybody off. It's extra sad because Kate was a Last Child, just like Jenny.

"You're lucky, Sarathi, remember that." Momma's squeezing Sarathiel to her and when Momma squeezes you, even your Book can feel it. "You get to live your own life."

Sarathiel shrugs and gives the kind of smile that means she doesn't want to argue. She kisses Momma on the cheek and bustles back towards the kitchen. Sarathi's only hope of becoming an Archivist again is if one of us dies, or retires, and that almost never happens.

"I hope I get to dream one day," I say, only partially because I know Momma will like it.

"Me too, honey." Then Momma leans towards me and whispers, "Once, Sam fell asleep in her office before I could disconnect, and she had a dream about eating Jalebi! She's never even *had* Jalebi!"

We laugh together and I keep pretending that I don't feel bad for my Momma's Book.

💾

Jenny wasn't paying attention to Ms. Houston for several reasons. One reason was that Ms. Houston was talking about the Scrivener's Arc *again*, and another reason was that Remmie Boyl had gotten a haircut.

Remmie's hair was short now, and shaved all the way to the tops of her ears. There was something about Remmie's ears that was making Jenny feel like she was being tickled on the inside. The back of Remmie's neck looked soft and fuzzy and freckled and Jenny wanted to touch it.

Remmie turned around, and Jenny focused on her social studies textbook so hard her face got hot and her eyes started to water.

"Jenny Winslow." Ms. Houston had impeccable timing. She always knew when it was the absolute worst time to call on Jenny. "Jenny, can you tell us why the Scrivener's Arc is more important now than ever before?"

Jenny looked at Ms. Houston—and definitely not at Remmie Boyl burning in her peripheral vision—and said, "Because we're Last Children."

"Please elaborate." Ms. Houston had to know, right? She *had* to know this was torture.

Jenny took a deep, shaky breath and balled her hands into fists. "The earth's resources are depleted. The human race is dying here, so we need to leave. But the Scrivener's Arc was made so that we would always remember what it was like to live here."

Ms. Houston looked around the room. "Anything to add, people?"

Remmie's hand shot up and Jenny wished she was dead. Or swimming.

"Because we're the last generation on Earth, we each get assigned an Archivist and they kinda watch us and record everything that happens to us and everything we think and everything." Remmie was talking to the whole class, but her eyes kept darting towards Jenny.

Jenny *really* wished she was swimming right now.

For the rest of the day, every time Jenny thought about Remmie her whole body would get overheated and she'd start fidgeting. So, she'd close her eyes for a bit and pretend she was swimming to calm down.

She only let herself think about Remmie on purpose when she went to bed. She imagined touching Remmie's neck. She imagined Remmie had come to her last meet and watched her win, only Coach and Mom weren't there. Remmie was the only one in the stands, except...

There was someone else, too. A weird looking girl with a shaved head and a jumpsuit full of holes. She looked like she was wearing a silver crown. She waved at Jenny, and smiled, and her smile was too big for the rest of her. She opened her mouth and—

💾

I cry out in pain. I hadn't prepared for disconnect, and it shoots through me like an electric shock.

Archivist Marigold-Jay-359, reidentify.

Everything still hurts, and I'm crying a bit. "Z-Zophiella Raqib."

Archivist Marigold-Jay-359, present three personal characteristics.

"I—" I'm not allowed to use the same ones two disconnects in a row. "My favorite food is pickles and cheese-toast. M-my Momma's name is Dina. I... I want to dream someday."

I shouldn't have said that last one.

Your three are accepted.
Zophi, why did you fail to disconnect?

The suit sits me up, and once my hands are free I'm wiping tears and snot off my face. "It was an accident."

Don't worry, Zophi.
Accidents happen.
The pain will pass.

The Scribe sounds kind, but I bet this is going on my permanent record.

When we meet at the Canteen, I tell Momma about Jenny's crush on Remmie, and she makes cooing noises that are a little mean. Lately, I try to never tell Momma anything bad about Jenny.

Sarathiel comes by to take our plates and I stand up to help her, telling Momma I'll be right back.

"When Kate was dying, did she ever dream about you?" I ask when we're far enough away.

Sarathiel makes a face and I realize my question was insensitive. "I'm sorr—"

"How did you know?"

Sarathiel and I huddle near the kitchen window where the dirty dishes go, and I whisper over the sound of the dishwasher.

"Towards the end..." Sarathiel's shy, soft voice is a little tight. "We could talk. I told her my name."

I need to head back to Momma before she thinks I'm being weird. "Thank you, Sarathi."

As I walk back towards our table, I look over at the long, squat viewing port that runs the length of the canteen. It's only just earthrise, and the blue dollop on the horizon looks like a water droplet when it gathers on your skin.

💾

Jenny and Remmie smiled at each other on the bus to school.

Jenny thought her body was going to peel away and a new, better, bigger body was going to climb out of it. A body that was big enough to contain Jenny and all her feelings. She felt so big.

Her new bigness was part of what gave her the confidence to raise her hand in Ms. Houston's class and ask, "Um, Ms. Houston? Has anyone ever met their Archivist?"

Ms. Houston looked pleased, for once. "Jenny, that is a wonderful question! Does anyone know the answer?"

A bunch of hands flew up, which made Jenny feel a little stupid, but then—

Remmie Boyl didn't wait to get called on by Ms. Houston. She turned around in her chair, and looked directly at Jenny. "Sometimes Archivists mess up. Like, they don't get out of our heads in time before we fall asleep and then we can sometimes see them or feel them or whatever. It's not supposed to happen."

"That's right, Remmie," Ms. Houston said, "but please wait to be called on."

Later, on the playground, Remmie came up to Jenny and offered her some of her gummies. "Did you see your Archivist, or what?"

Jenny took the gummies and held them in her hot, sweaty hand. "Um, yeah. Maybe. In a dream." She was *not* going to tell Remmie what the dream was about.

"What did she look like?"

Jenny shrugged, trying to remember the girl from her dream. "She was like...bald. And like, super ashy. She looked sick."

"Did you try to talk to her?

Jenny shook her head. She was so happy Remmie was talking to her, but at the same time really wished she'd go away. The gummies had completely melted in her hand and she was scared to open it now. "No, she looked like she was gonna say something, but then... I don't remember. I think the dream ended, or changed, or whatever."

That night, Jenny tried to fall asleep as fast as possible, hoping she'd dream about her Archivist again so she could talk to Remmie about it.

She dreamt she was waiting for Remmie on the playground, but it was the weird bald girl who showed up instead. She was shorter than Jenny and kind of soft all over, but skinny. She smiled her giant smile and said, "Hi, I'm Zophi."

Jenny didn't know what to say. "Hi?"

She felt weirdly guilty, and didn't know why. It felt weird that Zophi knew about Remmie. Jenny didn't like looking at Zophi.

"You don't have to feel bad about anything, Jenny. I like being your Archivist. I love it when you swim."

Jenny smiled shyly. "Me too." She thought for a bit about what to say, and then asked, "What do you like to do?"

Zophi looked surprised, but pleased. "I like to draw. Mostly people, but also animals. I'm not that bad."

"That's cool. I can't draw at all. Like, not even a circle," Jenny giggled, and the sick-looking Archivist girl named Zophi laughed with her. The grommets, the metal-plated holes in her jumpsuit, clinked as she shook. Jenny could see that under them there were grommets in Zophi's body, too. Points of connection. The crown was a circlet with narrow metal rods that were connected directly to Zophi's skull.

Jenny wanted to look away, but she was afraid to hurt Zophi's feelings.

"I wanted to ask you," Zophi began and opened her mouth, but then her too-big eyes widened further and she screamed and screa—

💾

Archivist Marigold-Jay-359, reidentify.

I can't breathe. My whole body's cramping, convulsing, and there's pressure building in my head because I *can't breathe.*

Archivist Marigold-Jay-359,
REIDENTIFY.

Finally, I gasp, and cough out. "Z-zh-zz—"

Zophi, why did you fail to disconnect?

"Z-zzz-Zophhhhiella," I manage, sobbing and shaking. "Raqib."

Zophi, the Scribe's voice sounds gentle again.

Why did you fail to disconnect?
It hurts you to be disconnected by force.

"I'm s-s-sssorry." The suit hasn't fully released me yet, so I can't reach up to wipe my face. "It was an acci—"

Don't lie, Zophi.

"I wanted," I sniffle. My mouth is full of salt. "I wanted to talk to Jenny."

You know you're not supposed to do that.

"I know."

Have a good night's rest, Zophi.

The suit finally releases me and I stumble out. I lay curled up on the floor until I feel strong enough to walk to the canteen and meet Momma.

She frowns when she sees me. "You okay, honey?"

"Tired from Jenny's swim practice. How's Sam?"

"A walking disaster, as usual," Momma sighs, smiling. "But her peace lily looks like it might flower, so she's happy about that."

I smile and force myself to eat. "That's nice."

Momma watches me for a bit. "Yeah. It is nice."

💾

"That is *sick.*" Remmie took a sip of soda and passed it to Jenny. "Like, actual holes in her arms and head?"

Jenny nodded. "Like she was part of a machine." She tried not to think about Remmie's lips and her lips touching the same bottle.

"You should ask her way more questions next time." Remmie's shoulder rubbed against Jenny's.

"I will."

That night, when the girl showed up, looking gray and small and full of holes, Jenny asked, "Zophi, can you tell me more about yourself?"

Zophi's face lit up, but she smiled uncertainly. "Sure, but there's not much to tell. I, um, my full name is Zophiella Raqib and my favorite color's light blue. Like...like earthrise." Zophi blushed, and continued. "My Momma's name is Dina. Um, I'm three months older than you." She laughed, embarrassed. "I don't know what else to say."

"Tell me what it's like being an Archivist, what's it like living on the Scrivener's Arc?"

Zophi shrugged, still smiling, but then her face went blank, her eyes rolled up, and she—

💾

*Archivist Marigold-Jay-359,
you have been retired.*

I know there's pain, but I can't feel it.

Goodbye, Zophi.

I can't feel anything. I'm sinking backwards into sleep. Real sleep, not rest. I'm floating in Jenny's pool.

I'm dreaming.

I dream about Jenny.

I dream she remembers my name. My mother's name. And that I like to draw.

I dream that she remembered me. She remembered I was her Archivist. She remembered...I was.

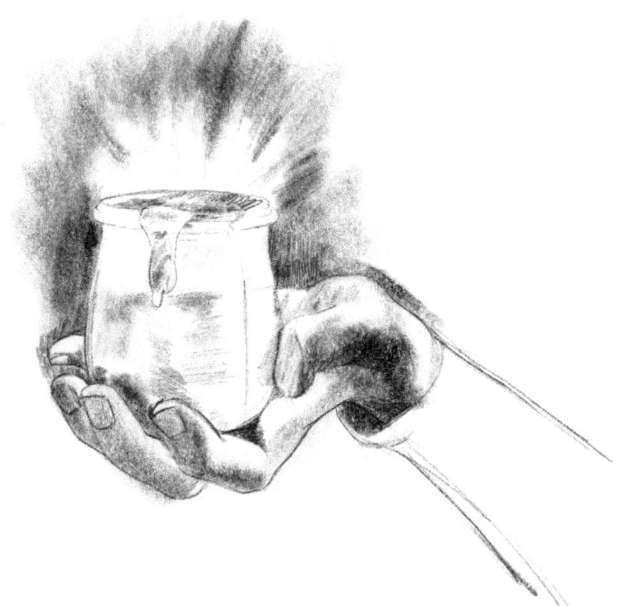

HARRIS COVERLEY

A TASTE OF THE SWEET STUFF

After being buzzed through, the new intern came into my office and introduced himself. "Mr. Curtis, Azif Rahsaan, tertiary technician. Reporting for duty, sir."

I leaned over my desk and shook his hand. "Mr. Rahsaan, I appreciate a little formality now and then, but this is a state institute, not a military base. Too much 'sir'-ing will makes us tense. Just call me Paul."

"Yes sir," he replied. "I mean—Paul, sir."

He was nervous. Still young, about twenty-five, with something of a schoolboy's haircut. His knees were knocking slightly.

I decided the best way to familiarize him with our work was not to plant him straight in the lab, but to take him up to the launch floor and show him the process in action. The building is incredibly tall for a rural structure, so it took awhile to reach the top in the lift.

As we stood there in the claustrophobic stainless steel chamber, I asked him: "So, what was your field again?"

"At Morrex-Bourne it was femtorobotics and hybrid engineering. Specialising in synthetic arachnids."

"Mechanical spiders?"

"In essence, yes."

"Why on earth would they need those?"

"I was never entirely sure. They didn't brief us on it. Military operations of one type or another, but I really don't know."

"Why leave the private sector? That's where the money is."

"I felt like I was going nowhere, and I wanted to contribute something to the public good, I guess."

Admirable. Maybe not the best career move, but admirable.

After a minute's journey we got to the launch floor. It's a large platform in the sky, open to the air at one end, the other end covered with thousands of little automated chambers and maintenance tunnels—"The Hive." The steel floor has hundreds of long grooves cut into it, little walkways, opening into shallow bays towards the edge. The other two walls are transparent, contained beneath a reinforced concrete roof covered with fluorescent lighting. The man in the street would have no idea

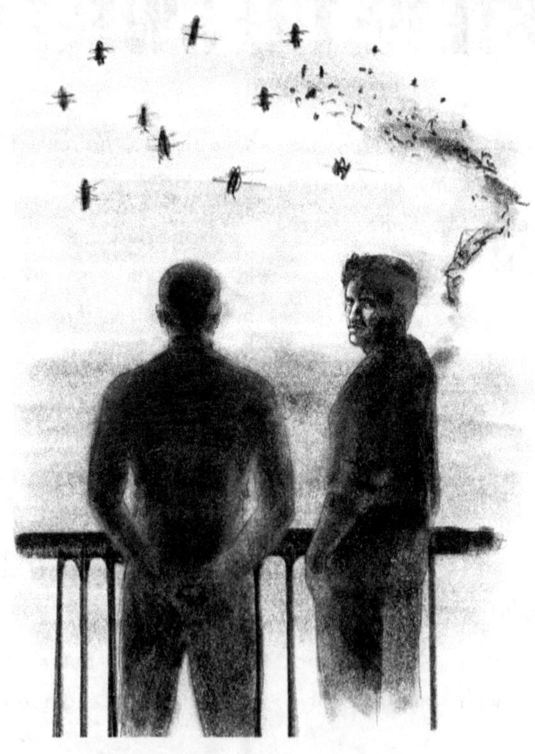

A TASTE OF THE SWEET STUFF

what to make of it. My father—when he visited—certainly did not.

Luckily for us, as we walked onto the observation deck, the drones were returning.

Thousands upon thousands of them came across in great, synchronised, metallic swarms, blocking out and fracturing the morning light. Their collective humming sounded like a giant, other-worldly blender.

They made long, martial lines in the grooves along the platform as they entered, and millions of tiny ceramic legs slowly but surely made their way back into their catacombs. There, the technical staff—who the young man beside me would soon be joining—directed repairs made by microscopic arms, drills, soldering irons, and nanobotic fluids.

I turned to look at Azif. He was utterly mesmerised, speechless. He had surely seen the instructional videos the institute had sent him, but to see it in person was an experience many would pay for. It did not bother me, of course. Not these days. It was all pretty...routine.

When the last swarm came in and made their way to repairs, I turned to Azif. "The next Legion goes out in three hours. The whole process lasts three months of the year. The rest of the time we do what the wonks call 'pure research.' It's mostly just tinkering."

"And this base serves the entire region?" Azif shouted over the continuing hum of drones and the rustle-crunch of repair mechanisms.

"Well, the area in the East Midlands we've been allotted by the central office," I replied. "Just think of it: without us and the drones, for a fifty mile radius there wouldn't be a single pollinated flower, potato, apple, pear, or onion. The landscape would be dead and colourless. If the Legion system shut down the world over, humanity would go extinct within a year—unless we switched to bananas and soybeans for the rest of our lives."

"And this has been going on since the Great Extinction?"

"Nearly twenty years now. Farmers pay their fertilisation tax and the local councils receive it in grants. And to think all of this almost never happened if it wasn't for the Dearth of '23 scaring the government into funding it. I left a good doctoral programme to work on the initial project, but I didn't care that much. It was engineering at its most radical. I've been here since the beginning, and I still love it."

"It's fascinating!" he yelled. Most

of the drones had returned to the Hive, and the *clank-crunch-grind* of the repair process had become unbearable, so I moved us back into the lift.

"It's the most marvelous triumph of human ingenuity. They do everything bees once did, except make honey."

An updraft from the swarms had disheveled Azif's boyish hair, and he was trying to claw it back into position "Could they, though? Make honey? I mean, if you programmed them to?"

"It's possible," I replied. "But there's no research money for it. Attempts to make it in enzyme vats produced something like corn syrup, but somehow even more disgusting. Sorry to say, honey is as dead as the bees that made it."

"I've never had any honey," he said. "What was it like?"

I knew it was one of *those times.* An occasion where I could have been restrained and kept the "secret" to myself. But I was too much of a blabber-mouth, I guess. I also liked the guy. He was curious, but not in an arrogant way. He cared about his work, and ours.

I took him back to my office, rather than back to the lab One of the major perks afforded to the co-director of a scientific organisation such as mine is a small kitchenette in one's office corner.

I boiled the kettle, preparing Azif a cup of tea (myself, a black coffee) before opening the paint-stripped mini-fridge and getting out a sliced loaf of bread. I always liked several slices of toast throughout the day. They kept me going without the need for a full lunch.

I put two slices in the toaster and put the loaf back. At the back of the top shelf of the mini-fridge, behind the butter and assorted jams, there was a small unmarked quarter-full glass jar of yellowish gloop. I brought it out and showed Azif.

"What is it?" he asked.

"You might not believe me if I told you," I said, holding it aloft.

"Try me."

I liked this emerging spirit he was starting to show me.

"You must promise not to tell anyone about this, outside or inside the institute."

"Promise?"

"You must promise me or I must end this conversation now and send you to your work."

"I promise, Paul. With all my heart."

I looked up at the jar in my hand.

"This, my son," I said to him, "is grade-A honey. Fresh as it was twenty years ago."

A TASTE OF THE SWEET STUFF

"Forgive me, but that's impossible," Azif said, crossing his arms.

"My mother bought this jar for me to go in the kitchen cupboard of my new flat in December of 2022. I didn't even realise I still had it until two years later when I moved out."

"But, how?"

"It never goes off. At least I don't think it does. It always tastes good for me."

"And you've kept it this long? While still eating it?"

The toast popped up. I put them on separate plates, but did not butter them.

"If you moderate yourself," I said, "you can preserve anything for a long time. I've been eating a little dabble once a month for the past fifteen years. I usually have it on a Friday after what I feel to be a good week's work."

"This is a tad ridiculous..." He then noticed the two plates of toast.

"Are you...?"

"Only those whom I feel deserve it get a taste of the sweet stuff—and only once, mind."

"I can't," he said. "Look how little is left!"

"All things die, Azif," I told him. "If a meteor struck the Earth tomorrow and burned the lot of us, this honey would bubble and boil in the jar and burst out, having missed a final chance to be appreciated."

I removed the lid off the jar.

"Isn't this illegal?" he asked.

"To be honest, I don't know, and I don't much care. Here, have a smell."

He leaned forward gingerly and rumpled his nostrils.

"Sweet," he whispered. "And sickly, but only a little."

I got out a butter knife and gently inserted it into the goo. I ladled out a small blob of the stuff, carefully avoiding spillage, and spread it across the crusty surface. I scraped as close as I could, until there was virtually nothing left on the blade, before wiping the knife clean.

"Why do that?" he asked. "Isn't it wasteful?"

"I don't want any crumbs in my honey, do I?" I replied with a smirk, before repeating the process with the other slice.

When I finished I handed him his plate and we sat down in front of my desk. He picked up the slice, smelt it again, and looked at me.

"It's not poisonous lad," I said, suppressing a laugh. "Eat it like any other slice of toast. But you must let it slide honey-side down across your tongue. That's the biting point."

We took our first bites in tandem. I crunched away and it was as good as always. He seemed confused, but he carried on chewing. As scientists we of course had poor table manners, and my office was quickly filled with the sound of open-mouthed chewing.

We were on our respective third bites when I realised he seemed to just be chewing and swallowing without savouring.

"Remember," I said between chews, "let the honey *slide* across the tongue. Force it if need be."

He took another bite and he seemed to manoeuvre his mouth around to follow my instructions. His expression changed. It wasn't ecstasy—I never would expect that—but suddenly his face, relatively cold before, filled with warmth. He smiled and a few crumbs fell from his lips.

We sat in silence (well, not talking that is—there was plenty of crunching going on) while we finished our slices. Azif handed me his plate and I piled them up on the sideboard to wash later. I remembered to put the jar back in the fridge.

When I turned around Azif's expression had shifted from overwhelming satisfaction to sadness.

"What's the matter?" I asked, sitting back in the chair opposite him.

"Is that it, then?" he replied.

"I'm afraid so. I want to make it last as long as humanly possible. I was wasteful at the beginning, and I strive to savour it to make up for lost servings. I'm sorry. No extra portions."

"Why?" he asked.

"Why what?"

"Why give me any at all?"

I got up out of the chair and sat back behind my desk.

"Azif," I said to him, folding my hands like in prayer, "I like to think we work miracles here. Because of what we and our inventions do, we are able to feed England and indeed the world a healthy, balanced diet, while also filling in a hole in the bio-pyramid. But we are not gods.

"We were foolish in not dealing with the Great Extinction when it was happening, and by the time we started to figure out solutions it was too late. The jar of honey in that fridge is like a little piece of the Garden of Eden. It's a reminder of our failures, but it's still just a touch of heaven, a little piece of living past. I just thought that if you're going to work here you ought to have a taste of

      A TASTE OF THE SWEET STUFF

that past, to see where we stand."

"It's been a privilege," said Azif, standing up. I almost thought he was going to salute me.

"Privilege? Maybe," I said. "Think of it as a bit of culinary luck."

"Do you think there's any other honey going around anywhere?" he asked.

"I hear rumours—there's always rumours—of this or that being sold here and there, but it's always black smoke and cracked mirrors. I know for a fact they preserved some in the seed bunker in Svalbard, and that a few agricultural institutes and museums have samples. I went to the Natural History Museum on holiday in New York a few years ago, and they had a tiny test tube of the stuff in the insect exhibit, probably behind bulletproof glass."

"I see."

I began to feel that I had made a mistake. Giving him that taste may have bummed him out a bit. This had backfired once before. I decided to get him straight into his duties.

"Well," I started, "we can't bugger about all day. I want you go up to the technical floor, Level 5, Room 4A, and talk to Carlos Holmes. He'll assign you a work desk and you'll be just in time to observe and start to learn the prep for

the next Legion."

"Yes Paul, I'll go right away," he said. Azif went to my door, then turned back.

"Erm, Paul?" he asked.

"Yes," I said, fiddling with a file on energy expenditure on my desk.

"What you said about a world without pollination. Would it really be so bad having to live off bananas and soybeans?"

His question took me by surprise. I had been using that joke for several years, and had never really thought of its broader implications. I knew I needed to come up with something or I would look foolish.

"Erm, well Azif," I said, "it wouldn't be a very interesting diet, would it?"

"No, I guess not." He smiled a proper smile for the first time since I met him. He seemed satisfied, and left me to my work. I had managed to gain his trust.

Although I knew I had at least ten reports to file before three o'clock, I took the time to lean back in my chair and close my eyes. I laughed to myself a little.

It was all a fake of course. The jar of "honey" in question was just a portion of the cheapest and blandest golden syrup available, mixed with a little honey essence I had long since borrowed from my grandmother's cake-making box.

I had given that speech half a dozen times, with little variations. It got better on each occasion.

Give them a little incentive, and they'll spin you straw into gold. I felt like a bastard sometimes, but that was the nature of organising a workplace.

I did have a jar of honey on my person once, and I know exactly where it is. It is in the Svalbard seed bunker, contained in the Paul Curtis Chamber. Technically, it is only being preserved there in case of some global disaster. I still legally own it, in fact. All I need now is the right enzyme composite, and the right kind of produce vat, and I might just be able to make myself the richest food magnate in the world.

And before you do, do not think of me in *that* way. I still love all my work. I just want something to show for it.

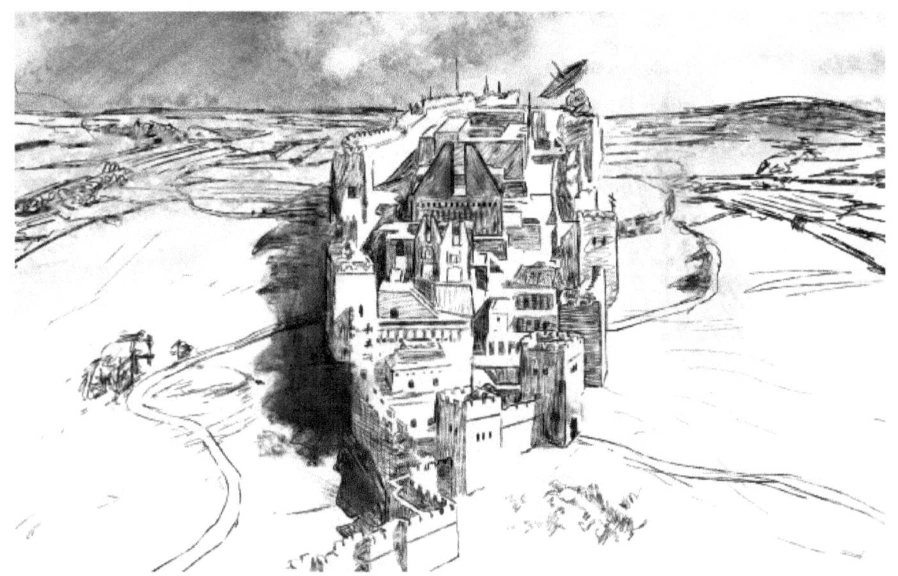

STEVE DuBOIS

PRODIGAL

The Lucan sun still lay beneath the horizon when our eldest, Hezekiah, requested an audience.

My husband, Shadrach, was not at his best. His eyes were the harsh crimson of Lucan soil and his long beard was a rumpled tangle. He and the other men had celebrated late into the night. We women had been up late too, preparing the feast so the locally-grown produce would not kill all who consumed it. The butchery of the fatted calf added additional hours. Such a prodigal waste.

As ever, no labor on our part could purge the food of the rancid tang of iron. Every bite at a Lucan table tastes of blood.

Hezekiah had abstained from celebration. His eyes were clear. He stood straight and unruffled. "Father," he said, "I ask for my inheritance."

Shadrach blinked. He sat cross-legged on the mat, his brow furrowed.

"I am...surprised by this request. You have seen the consequences of your brother's irresponsibility. Just yesterday, you saw him stumble up the road towards us, tears on his face, his pride in tatters, his inheritance wasted. Is this the course you wish to pursue? Dissolution, avarice, and ruin? Off to Bradbury, like him, to dice and carouse with pirates, traders, and whores?" He raised an eyebrow.

There could, of course, be no thought of Hezekiah in such an environment. My mind flitted back to his childhood, to him and his brother on the red dunes. Balthazar, forever toddling off towards trouble. Hezekiah in his wake, watching out for him, herding him back.

"No, father," Hezekiah replied. "I want to build a farm of my own."

Shadrach spread his arms wide. "But you have that here! All that I have is yours! Have I not always said so? Did I not prove it yesterday, in the way I treated your brother?"

"A farm on Earth," Hezekiah replied.

I was, in truth, as stunned as my husband. It was only after a long pause that he managed to reply. "You jest."

"I do not." Hezekiah's face was serene. "I have studied on it. I know the land. I know the crops. I know the methods. And you cannot say that you have ever met a man who can work harder, or more ably, than I."

"Ability is not the issue!" Shadrach exclaimed. "You will be up against the devil himself! The people of the old world are immersed in hochmut. They seek only their own advancement. The love of family and community is alien to them. They do not take what the land gives willingly, but demand ever more. They rape the earth with fertilizers and pesticides, and grind her in the gears of their *machines!*" He spat the word as if it were the vilest of curses.

"Machines, father? Like the rocket that brought our forefathers here?"

"A blessing. A dispensation from the Lord to liberate us from bondage among the heathens. To protect our ways from being drowned in the economic tide. To bring us closer to God. Technology is not sinful except when it separates us from the Lord. This is known to you." He paused. "You were born of this world, Hezekiah. You do not know what it is to stand on Earth. How that world weighs on a man, saps his strength with every step. You cannot stand under the burdens it imposes."

"There are therapies," Hezekiah replied. "Exercises. It is not unknown for those born on low-gravity worlds to acclimate. And I am strong."

"Yes, strong. But wise?" Shadrach shook his head in amazement. "I had always thought so. I had always imagined your brother the foolish one."

"As had I," Hezekiah answered. "But now I know he was far wiser than I. Every day I worked our shrunken patch, I thought him a wastrel. I thought he had gambled and lost." A long pause. "And then, father, yesterday, I saw him reach out to you—and saw you run to embrace him. I saw that he had gambled nothing. He knew what I did not. He knew you. He knew that the price of his pleasures was, in the end, no price at all."

My son's jaw was tightly set. At length, Hezekiah spoke. "I was angry with him in that moment, yes. But I was proud of him as well. He comes away from his adventure rich with memories; I come away from my labors with itching eyes and calloused palms. My brother is no fool. He knows what a farmer must." And here Hezekiah looked long at his father. "The nature of the land he works."

He licked his lips, which were chapped and cracked from long hours in the fields, and deployed the argument he'd been saving. "I never took *rumspringa*, father. I never saw the point. But I daresay I see it now. Shall we call it that? My long-delayed *rumspringa*?"

A long, barren silence. At length, Shadrach stood. "Go, then," he said.

"Not in anger, but with your father's blessing."

I felt a dagger pierce my heart, but Shadrach never noticed, never so much as spared me a glance. Instead, he spread his arms wide, the picture of fatherly grace and charity. Hezekiah walked slowly into them, and the two embraced.

My son's eyes met mine over his father's shoulder, met me where I sat cross-legged upon the floor in my long skirts. I knew how I must have looked to him—a withered thing. Hair straying from under my bonnet, a grey wisp before my eyes, careworn fingers folded before me. Nonetheless, my son's eyes beheld me with love.

"Do not think, Hezekiah, that the endless gulfs of space are sufficient to separate you from my compassion. On that day when you come marching up the road—the dust of two worlds upon you, broken by Earth's relentless pull—then, as with your brother, I will gather you into my loving arms again. Do not doubt it! Your home is here."

Shadrach paused to think. "The logistics, of course, will be formidable. Our family's savings will purchase you a berth on an Earth-bound freighter, I suppose. But the sale of the land that would have been yours? That will take some time. The money will be forwarded."

"Thank you, father. You are just as well as merciful." Worry creased Hezekiah's brow. "Still... your plot will be much reduced by the sale. And with so much of the harvest used up in last night's celebration ..."

Shadrach waved off the concern. "The Lord will provide," he insisted. "Do not forget, Sarai's share remains!"

It was true. Our law required that a portion of a man's wealth be set aside for his wife, should he predecease her.

"Her blessed tenth." He turned upon me, beaming. "Ah, what an honor, to have a tenth! A share as great as the Lord's own!"

I reflected a shadow of his smile back at him—a tenth part, perhaps—and he was content. He turned back to our son. "And we shall have Balthazar beside us to work the plot. The Lord will provide." So spoke Shadrach unto our son, giving his blessing to Hezekiah's descent into Hell.

I said nothing. But I thought to myself: *Two sons I have borne this man, and two sons he has lost me. I have at long last reclaimed Balthazar, only to lose Hezekiah, so that my husband can hope someday to once again play his favorite role and revel in his own magnificent love and forgiveness.*

I had beheld the previous day's events through the window of our domicile. Balthazar's tear-streaked return, Hezekiah in his anger... I had played no part. Yesterday's story had been that of a father and his sons.

I promised myself: *Today's story will be that of a mother.*

Our forefathers were Swartzentrubers, plain folk of the old style, but the stock was not pure. There were geneticists and ecologists—men of science. The desperation of Earth had made for strange bedfellows. The plain folk had been driven to the brink of extinction by competition. Mechanized agriculture and forever-increasing yields drove the prices of crops down, and down, and down again until even the prices of the tools they needed were beyond them.

The men of science, too, came to realize the error, as the dead zones at the mouths of rivers grew, as the tainted seeds contaminated those around them. Many came to realize the merit of the customs of the plain folk. So, they joined with our forefathers and sought out a world suited to a simpler way.

Luke is such a world. The wickedness of Earth cannot pursue us here, for Luke is an old world; erosion and entropy

PRODIGAL

have had their way with her, and the red soil is fine as talcum. It is as ubiquitous as the Lord's justice; no filter can keep it out entirely, and no motor runs long under its corrosive influence.Our men wear masks in the fields, and goggles over their eyes, and bear simple tools in their hands. Our women sweep the dirt constantly from the floors, and wash with whenever water is available. But we are forever unclean.

It had been thought, at first, that the unique properties of Lucan soil would bring forth a bountiful harvest. And indeed, it was so. The crops, as modified by our scientists, were rich with nutrients. It was not until that first harvest feast—a meal at which, the histories say, our forefathers forgot to give thanks to the Lord—that we discovered the price of our hubris. Men collapsed to their knees, retching, their heads spinning, the corners of their mouths cracking.

Hypervitaminosis A, they called it. Not poisoning, a surplus of the stuff of life. Too much of a good thing. Prodigal. Many died before our scientists were able to synthesize an antidote from the yolks of eggs.

And so, as God intended when he cast Adam and Eve from the Garden, we labor in the fields. With the greatest effort, our men cultivate the hybrids our forefathers designed, tasting always of iron. Women prepare the table, treating the fruits and vegetables with the sacred seasonings that prevent us from being overwhelmed by God's bounty. Thus are we reminded, at every meal, of the wages of sin. Thus is *demut* maintained.

It was in the spirit of *demut* that Shadrach had come to court me, in the morning of our youth, holding his hat before him. Humble, yes. But so handsome! And so full of piety, of God's mercy. His kindness resounded in every action, from our earliest chaperoned walk to our eventual marital bed. Hand in hand by the fire, he would read aloud to me from a precious collection of books brought from Earth. The Bible, yes, but also Bunyan, and Milton, and especially Shakespeare. And, yes, his kindness showed in his literal cartwheel of joy when I told him I was with child, puffs of Lucan dust trailing in his wake.

To carry a child is an easy thing on Luke, for this world does not bind us to it as Earth does. But to bear a child is another thing entirely, for without the weight of Earth, the womb quickens strangely. Some babes come forth stillborn, others as monsters. We do not complain. We went forth from the Garden in sin, and there is always a price to pay.

Hezekiah's birth was eighteen hours of agony. By the time he had emerged into the world in a wash of scarlet pain, I was nearly insensate. Yet the midwives tell me that in my stupor, I clutched him to my breast with feverish intensity. So much so that my husband, for all his strength, could not pluck our son from my arms.

A love to rival his own.

Shadrach had made a point to involve himself as actively as he could in Hezekiah's upbringing—the changing of his swaddling clothes, the soothing of his midnight cries. I believe that his one great regret was that he could not nurse the babe himself.

Two years later came Balthazar. This time, it took two full days. The pain was such that I begged the Lord to take me, yet every time I thought He would, I felt Shadrach's love pulling me back.

Finally, the child came. As I suckled my son in a blissful haze, the midwife told me, "You are lucky to be alive. But make no mistake, even if you survive, you are ruptured beyond repair. You will never bear another child."

My husband sat at my bedside. His eyes never shifted from his newborn son. He absently laid a hand on my forehead. "Have no concern, Sarai," he intoned. "I forgive you."

Hezekiah had long since disappeared down the road to Bradbury when Balthazar finally emerged on unsteady legs into the light. The sun neared its zenith, and a light breeze shuffled Luke's red dust through the fields, around gnarled trunks and narrow stalks. There stood Balthazar, wayward and wild, irresistibly beautiful, hair golden and eyes green. He winced in the light, his face showing the after-effects of the previous night's celebration. But his eyes held no trace of shame.

Our stock is not pure and sometimes a seed grows wild. Balthazar, with his easy smile and laughing eyes is loved by all. How the fieldhands danced to see him returning! How the women of Bradbury must have mourned to see him go!

But, if I am honest, *demut* is not in him. I raised him as best I could, attempted to correct his waywardness, to impose consequences—only to be countermanded by his father. Shadrach, ever eager to demonstrate that a father's love can exceed a mother's. Sometimes a seed grows wild. The path which leads to the Lord is steep and rocky, and Balthazar is forever seeking a simpler way.

I watched through the window as Balthazar emerged into the light and found his father waiting with a hand-plow.

"Where is Hezekiah?" he asked.

Shadrach shook his head sadly. "Gone," he said. "But only for a time. Soon, you and I shall celebrate his return, as he and I celebrated yours. In the meantime," he said, proffering the grips of the plow, "you are returned to the fold, and the Lord's work awaits us both."

Balthazar stared down at the device as if it were the Serpent itself. "Today, father? I am yet unwell. I was, perhaps, a bit excessive, last night, in celebrating."

Shadrach laughed. "Weren't we all!" His smile disappeared. "We are *all* unwell, son. Sick with pride, and with the rejection of His ways. It is work that makes us whole. Was that not your offer to me yesterday? To be taken into the household again, not as my son, but as one of my fieldhands?" Again, he proffered the plow. "No. You are always my son. Now and forever."

Balthazar licked his lips. "But, father-"

"And what a thing it is, to be my son!" Shadrach smiled broadly. "To be never beyond the grasp of my love, and of my mercy."

Balthazar looked up at him. And I thought, as I watched through the window, that his eyes were not those of a grateful supplicant, but those of an animal in a trap. "Surely, father," he stammered, "some acts must be beyond-"

"You are my son," Shadrach interrupted. "Were you a murderer, a sodomite, or an apostate, you would be my son still. Wherever you flee, my love would follow. If you were to descend into the very bowels of Gehenna, my love would reach inside and pluck you out. Nothing you do can place you beyond the scope of my mercy, Balthazar." His face was suddenly hard, and the word that followed was the sweep of an autumn scythe: "*Nothing.*"

And then cheer returned to Shadrach's countenance. "But to be of my family is to accept the demands of honest labor. It will be hard, son. Hard, for a time, as we seek to survive on what remains, with your brother's inheritance and yours lost to us. But we shall endure! You and I, together! The Lord will provide, so long as we prove worthy of him."

With great reluctance, Balthazar took the plow into his hands and set to work.

Every so often, there comes a traveler up the road from Bradbury. He walks with that floating, springing step of those accustomed to Earth's pull, and he seeks employment with us, in the fields. Someone back home told him that Earth's pull is lessened here, and that the workload is correspondingly lighter. So, he comes to Luke in search of lighter labor and an easy life.

And, in time, the fool learns what the mothers of Luke already know. He learns it the moment he seeks to plow a furrow and finds that pull absent—discovers that the work the Earth once did for him is now his own to perform. He learns it when he brings down a pick or a spade and finds that every bead of sweat saved in the lifting must be repaid on the descent, as his muscles must perform the work the world used to. They learn. Some stay. Most leave, poorer but wiser.

I watched through the window as my beloved Balthazar re-learned what he had forgotten. I saw him rub at his softened hands as the blisters rose. I watched my son drop to his hands and knees, and spew last night's leavings into a drainage ditch, heaving again and again. Yet his body knew that its sin was not purged. His stomach lurched, bringing up nothing. And I swept, and wove, and churned, and watched through the window, and wept.

And by sundown, he was gone. I cast my eyes aside for a moment—to the task before me, or perhaps up to the heavens to pray—and when they returned to the fields, my boy was gone. Gone up the road to Bradbury again, perhaps, or into the wilderness. None could say for certain, for none had seen him leave.

Before, Balthazar had decided that his father's mercy was a lesser blessing than his inheritance, and a dissolute life. This time, Balthazar had weighed his father's mercy against nothing at all. And he had chosen the latter.

Two sons I bore Shadrach, I thought. *And he has managed to lose me three.*

🖫

"A terrible thing, ingratitude," Shadrach said. "Our sons have much to learn." He chewed thoughtfully at the breadfruit I had prepared for him, a thin, red-brown trickle running from the corner of his mouth and down his chin. "We must redouble our efforts, Sarai. We must forgive them, and love them all the more. The Lord will show them their errors, and bring them back to us, in the fullness of time."

"Still, it will be hard. One fewer set of hands to work the fields, and with the dry season coming on..." Shadrach mused. "Another hired hand, perhaps? But what to hire him with? And the sale of Hezekiah's patrimony to arrange in the meantime. So much work ahead." He sighed. "A long day, Sarai. My feet ache terribly. I don't suppose...?"

I said not a word, but knelt before him, removing his shoes and kneading at the hard and blistered soles of his feet.

"Aaaaah...yes. Blessed mercy! The Lord is the relief of all pain. We must never be hesitant to praise Him for—yes, a bit lower, I think, down by the arch— all His effort on our behalf." He paused. "And now...hmmm. Odd. The pain, it seems, is...not in my feet..." He pressed a hand to his temple.

I continued to knead away, and spoke for the first time that day. "Yes," I said. "A dull throb, behind the eyes."

Shadrach stared. His hand went to his chin, rubbed at the rivulet, stared at his fingers. Every bite at a Lucan table tastes of blood.

He glanced at me—at the helpmate the Lord had provided him. He looked at the fruit—fresh from the Lord's own garden and, just this once, untainted by a woman's hand. He looked at me, and knew himself a sinner.

"I confess, husband," I said. "My soul is at war with itself, and I know not where to turn. But we are all in the hands of the Lord, and I have faith that he will show me the way."

"Dear God," he whispered. "Mercy, Sarai. The antidote."

I nodded. Releasing his feet, I reached into a pouch in my garment, and withdrew a tiny vial. I tossed it to him. He caught it in suddenly palsied hands, raised it to his lips, and quaffed it. Then he stared at me as the palsy intensified. "Not..." A pink foam had formed on his lips. "Not enough..."

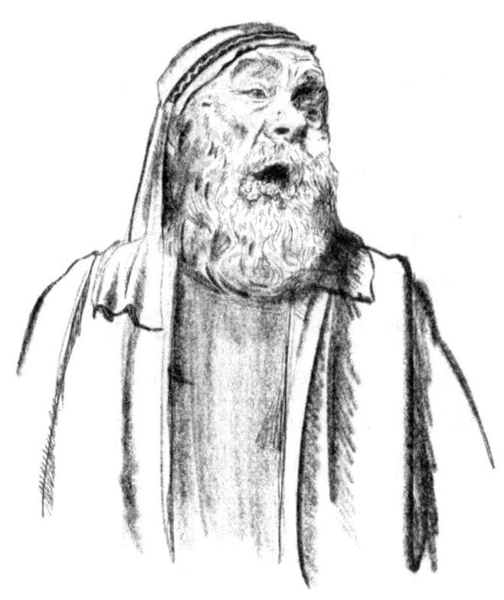

"A full tenth of the recommended dose. The Lord's own share." I took up his feet again, and rubbed at them. "You have spoken to me often of the Lord's infinite mercy. Almost as often as you have spoken of your own. Alas, I am but a woman. The knowledge the Lord grants by nature to a man, I must be shown." I stared over his quaking toes at his flushed and quivering face. "I pray now that the Lord will show me His mercy, and save my husband."

Over my husband's shoulder, I could

see the shelf on which the precious books from Earth were arrayed. The pages had yellowed over the years, grown fragile and crumbled at the corners. It had become necessary to commit the words to memory, lest they be lost.

My faith was imperfect. But my memory was excellent. My eyes returned to my husband's panicked countenance. I returned the favor he had once paid, and read aloud.

"The quality of mercy is not strained," I intoned. "It droppeth as the gentle rain from heaven upon the place beneath." I paused, rubbing at his feet. "On this world, husband, the rains come infrequently."

"Why, Sarai?" he asked, his eyes wide, muscles frozen, breath wheezing and rasping. "Was I...not always loving to you, and...to..."

"Your mercy was infinite," I replied, "as was your love. Too much of anything is prodigal. Excess in virtue is still excess, and pride in one's virtue is still pride. *Demut*, husband. An elegant sufficiency would have been wiser."

I released Shadrach's feet and rose. I removed a small towel from its position over the water tureen. I walked slowly back to my husband, closed his eyes, and placed the cloth over his face.

The message has been sent ahead to Bradbury, I thought. God willing, it will reach Hezekiah in time.

His patrimony, and my inheritance. The freedom to try, and to fail. To be weighed down, and to grow strong accordingly. To rise or fall by the sweat of his brow. The blessing of merciless-ness. Let it be sufficient, Lord. Let it be enough to bring him back to me.

Enough, even for three, should that by Thy will.

The bundle by the door held a large canteen and two days' rations. I hoisted it to my shoulder, stepped out into the haze, and went in search of my sons.

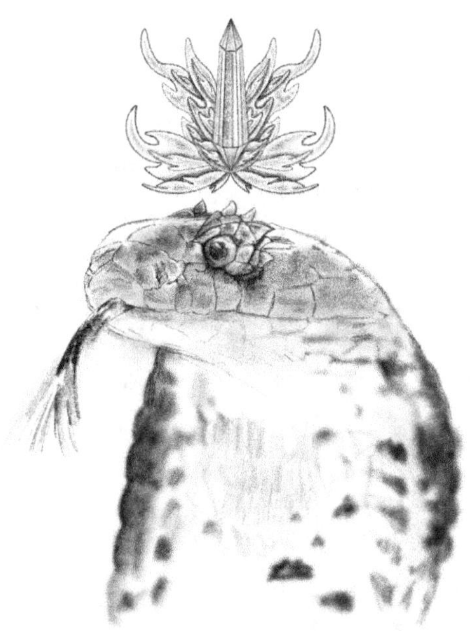

MAUREEN BOWDEN

SHAPESHIFTERS

The sun rose on England's Berkshire Downs, and the Great Wyrm, Naga, emerged from the Hill of the Beasts. The chalk figure carved into the hillside is known as the White Horse of Uffington, although it bears little resemblance to a horse. It depicts Naga herself—the work of her children in ancient times, before they disguised themselves in human form and spread throughout the land.

The Great Wyrm called to her children. In their true forms they crawled, flew, trotted and slithered to the hill, in response to her summons.

"Welcome," she said. "The human race is about to face the consequences of their abuse of the world. Earth is angry. She will have her revenge. Her tormentors will die. We will be safe. I will lead you through the dark recesses of our hill, deep beneath Earth's bones, until our day comes. Then we will return to the surface. You will take human form once more. You will mate with the few survivors. They will be the preservers of their race. Your descendants will honour Earth and she will nurture them."

She cast her eyes over the gathering of the beasts. "Some are missing."

The hawks squawked. "Our brother."

The reptiles hissed. "Our brother."

The wolves howled. "Our sister."

"Seek them out," Naga commanded. "Bring them here. Three nights from now we will enter the hill to await our day."

🖫

Kenny Bennett was what crime writers call an "old lag." He'd been in and out of clink, mostly in, for fifty years. Kenny had shared his cell with every stripe of humanity. He'd thought nothing could surprise him, but this latest specimen was a puzzle. He was short and wiry, with spiky dark hair and small, sharp eyes. Gave his name as "Hawk," expressed a wish for the top bunk, then fell silent.

Hawk lay there for hours, staring out of the cell's tiny barred window at the sullen winter sky. Kenny, on the bottom bunk, kept his nose in his porno mag, and minded his own business.

It was that way with Hawk and Kenny for some time, until one day in the exercise yard when three birds swooped and swirled above the inmates. Kenny had no idea what species, but they were large and black, with wingspans the size of hang-gliders, and ear splitting squawks that scared

the crap out of him. He'd never liked birds.

Hawk, however, watched the aerobatic display and smiled.

Kenny's heart pounded. He slumped down, leaned against a wall, and collected himself. Jack O'Neil, a screw who knew him from way back, hunkered down beside him. "You okay, Kenny?"

"Yeah," but I'll be better when I get out of this dump."

"You're up for parole soon, right?"

"Right. And this time I won't be back."

Jack lit a cigarette and passed it to him. "Better off staying where you are, old lad. We're in for a rough ride with this Hurricane Miranda blowin' up."

"Bloody daft names they give 'em. What's the point?"

"Keeps someone in a job, I suppose, but this one's been crashin' around the US, like a bleedin' bat outta hell. Now it's headin' over the Atlantic straight for us. You got family?"

"Only a granddaughter. My Beckie. Good girl. She'll look after me."

"You better look after her, too, y' hear?"

Later in the afternoon, back in the cell, the birds circled outside the window, beating their wings against the glass. Kenny backed as far away as possible. "What the fu-"

Hawk turned to him. "They've come for me."

The birds were still there when night fell. Kenny lay in the bottom bunk holding his blanket over his head. He whimpered in his sleep. All around he heard wings pounding, glass cracking, metal clanging and grinding. And then—silence, apart from a single whisper on the night wind:

"Shapeshifter."

Kenny rose, shivering in the cold morning air that blasted through the cell's broken window. The iron bars were bent and twisted. A black feather quivered among shards of shattered glass on the floor. Kenny was alone.

Rebecca Bennett—known to everyone who mattered as "Star"—passed through Walton Jail's public exit after visiting her grandfather. She took a deep breath, ridding her lungs of the prison's disinfectant smell—the stink of incarceration.

Star mounted her Harley Davidson, rode to the "Sons of Chaos MC" clubhouse, and parked in her usual space. The sunless Saturday afternoon sky was already darkening, and from the corner of her eye she glimpsed two or three writhing shadows, slithering across the gravel path and into the neglected privet hedge. She tried to shake off a sense of unease. Probably just grass snakes. Everything else appeared normal.

The Che Guevara poster adorned the clubhouse window. The life-size cardboard Cher cut-out stood on the porch. George Thorogood and The Delaware Destroyers' "Long Gone" rattled the rafters when she opened the door.

Star breathed easy. Yes, everything was normal.

Mocker was leaning on the bar in the party room.

"Where's Snake?" she asked him.

He shrugged, "He's your man, you find him."

"I don't appreciate the attitude, brother."

He backed off. The bikers didn't disrespect Star.

Jango, the vice-president, placed himself between them and slung his arm around her shoulders. "He's waiting for you in the backyard."

"Thanks."

As she moved away, Jango brushed her arm. "Star, he's in a mood."

"Noted."

She found Snake lounging on the wrought iron bench that had once stood outside the Maritime Museum until it had been transported, by persons unknown, to its present location.

The Sons' president was over six feet tall, and muscular. His hair hung in a waist-length braid, and a forked-tongue reptile tattoo spiralled up his left arm.

She sat beside him. He passed her his beer, and she took a swallow. "How's Kenny?" he asked.

"Good. He's up for parole in a couple of weeks. I hope the old fool learns to behave this time."

"Or learns not to get caught."

"Some hopes."

Two shadows slithered over the paving stones and disappeared through a crevice in the yard's brick wall. She shivered. "Those things are everywhere. What are they?"

"Vipers. They won't hurt you. They've come for me." She felt a chill down her spine. He'd told her about Naga and the Hill of the Beasts, warned her that this day was inevitable, but she'd thought it was all drug-fueled delusions.

"Take a ride with me." He led her to his bike, and she climbed on behind him. The throb and hum of the Harley soothed her. She clung to him and gave herself up to the moment.

They rode south of the city centre, following the line of the river, past the cast-iron shore (the "cazzie"), where rust from dead ships had turned the sand red.

They reached Otterspool Park. He leaned the bike against an ancient ash tree, spread his jacket on the grass, and pulled her down. After they'd made love they lay together, and kept each other warm, while vipers rustled in the bushes.

"How long will you be in the Hill?" she asked. "Years, or decades?"

He shook his head. "Months."

"Is that all it'll take?"

"Most of it. Yeah."

"I won't die."

"I know," he said, "and I'll find you."

"Look for me here, by the ash tree."

He helped her to her feet, picked up his jacket, and tore off the "President" patch from beneath The Sons' skull logo. "Give this to Jango. He's Prez now." He kissed her. "Time to go, Star."

She turned away, determined not to let him see her cry, and wheeled the bike away from the tree. She rode down to the banks of the river without looking back.

The incoming tide washed over the sand, and wept as the waves sang: "Shapeshifter."

There was one more thing she had to do. She waited until she was sure Snake would be gone before she rode back into the park. His clothes were scattered around the tree. She folded them into a bundle and placed them high in the branches, to keep them safe until he returned.

A silken sliver of...something lay discarded on the grass, shimmering in the moonlight. She stooped to touch it, and it disintegrated beneath her fingers, floating away like dust on the night wind. Snake had shed his skin.

Carl Woodhouse arrived home at dusk, and found a pack of wolves in his garden. He'd always dreaded this day. They ignored him as he drove into the garage and hurried into the house, slamming the door behind him.

He rang Morrighan. "Morri, don't come home. The garden's full of wolves." *Silence.* "Morri, did you hear me? I said-"

"I heard you, Carl. They won't bother you. The Great Wyrm's sent them for me."

"I know. Stay with a friend till I can pick you up. We need to get the hell out of here."

"No. They'll find me anyway. If I don't come home tonight we'll never see each other again. I'll be there in an hour." She ended the call.

This couldn't happen. Had anyone told the human race it was about to die? He turned on the early evening BBC TV news.

Fiona Bruce was reporting that ten people had contracted bird flu in the English Midlands.

"The patients are being treated in an isolation unit in Birmingham City Hospital." Fiona looked worried. "The airport, railway routes and National Express coach station have been closed, and road blocks are in place, but there are fears that carriers of the disease have already left the city."

She turned to a studio guest, introducing her as Professor Laura Parry of the Imperial College School of Medicine. The professor said, "Anyone who has been in the Birmingham area in the last two weeks and is feeling unwell, is urged to seek medical attention."

Carl walked into the kitchen and poured himself a whiskey. Stay calm, he told himself. They'll have everything under control. He stared through the kitchen window. The garden was in darkness. Six pairs of yellow eyes stared back at him. He pulled down the blinds and swallowed his whiskey in one gulp.

He took his glass, and the bottle, into the living room, in time to see the TV weather forecast. Hurricane Miranda would hit Britain within the next twenty-four hours. Loss of life was expected. The emergency services would evacuate residents of the hardest-hit regions. He screamed at the TV, "Evacuated to where? Birmingham?"

He switched to Channel Four News. Krishnan Guru-Murthy was reading international news.

"Volcanologists report increased subterranean activity in Yellowstone Park. They warn that a major eruption, which could have global consequences, may be imminent." Krishnan looked as worried as Fiona. "The park officials have, however, stressed that there is no immediate danger."

Carl swallowed another whiskey and clicked the remote for BBC Four, hoping for a repeat of "Top of the Pops" 1975. Maybe some glam rock distraction.

Instead, Professor Brian Cox—who wasn't smiling for once—was wearing a fur-hooded anorak and standing in a snow-covered landscape. He also looked worried.

"The polar ice is melting at an accelerated rate," he said. "The oceans are swelling, and flooding low-lying land. This is not a prediction for the future. It's happening now."

Carl heard Morrighan's car pull into the drive. He turned off the TV, opened the door, and closed it behind her without looking into the garden. She threw herself into his arms.

"I won't go with them," she said, as he led her into the living room. "I promised I wouldn't leave you."

They sat together on the couch.

"We're going to die, Morri," he said. "Time's up for humans, but you don't belong here. Go back to your own people."

"No, we talked about this. We agreed we'd stay together."

He knew how stubborn she was, and how faithful. There was only one way to save her life, although it would tear him apart to do it. "I don't want you to stay. I haven't got much time left. I have to make the most of it. I can't do that if I'm worrying about you. Go with the wolves."

She pulled away from him and he saw the shock in her eyes.

"But you said you loved me."

"Humans say that to each other all the time. They lie. That's what they do."

She shook her head. "I don't understand."

"That's because you're not human. You're an animal, and animals can be deceptive, I know, but they don't lie the way humans do." He knew how much he was hurting her but he couldn't let her throw her life away for him.

"Even if you don't love me, I love you, and I won't leave you to die alone."

"Oh, I won't be alone. I'll be having as much fun with as much company as I can get, for as long as I can get it." He forced himself to laugh. "I might give that good-looking biker chick a try, the one that hangs out with the Sons of Chaos. I wouldn't mind having fun with her."

Morrighan said nothing. She made no attempt to stop him when he pulled her to her feet, and back to the door. Better to do this now before his resolve failed him.

He led her outside before letting go of her arm, and then he called to the wolves, "Here's your shapeshifter. Take her and go." The wolves circled her.

She looked into his eyes. He knew she was human enough to see through the lie, and he was glad. He walked back to the house, faced her, and raised his hand in farewell. She returned his wave. He walked inside and closed the door, so he wouldn't see her change.

The setting sun stained the clouds pink over England's Berkshire Downs. The beasts gathered at the foot of the hill. The Great Wyrm, Naga, led her children to safety, deep beneath Earth's bones, to await their day.

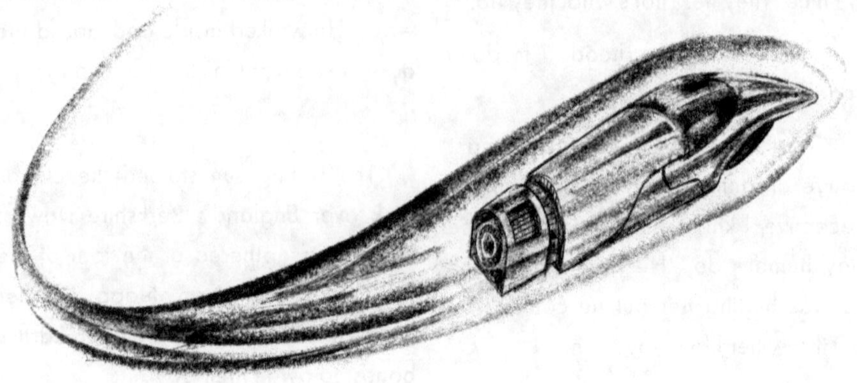

ANNA CATALANO

LAZARUS

The sound of my teeth gnashing together echoes in the Pod as I force my way through the newest 10,000 piece puzzle. I'm only a quarter done, but I can already tell that it's a postmodern piece of art by some guy no one really talks about anymore.

I'm tempted to leave it—to swipe the obnoxiously bright images off the ceiling, roll onto my stomach, and try and get some sleep. Is it even night? Who the hell knows anymore.

But to shut off the screen is to lie alone in the pitch black of the Pod, and I've never lasted long in that endeavor.

A frantic itch creeps back into my skin, the hot prickle of frustration and claustrophobia that I've become all too familiar with since my imprisonment. My fingers search for something to grab, a crack, a textured surface...anything but the cold, polished walls of the Pod.

Your name is Dante D'Avignon, I remind myself, willing the wave of panic from sweeping me under again. *Your sister's name is Fey. You live in the West District of Enneryl.*

I crack my knuckles hard enough to

bruise, focusing on the ache of my joints and the barely-there stink of my skin.

You shouldn't be in here.

Breathe in.

Throbbing knuckles.

Breathe out.

Flashing light of the touchscreen.

Breathe *in*.

The hot sting of sweat on my neck.

Breathe out.

The attacks are worse now that I'm in here. There's no sense of familiarity to ground me anymore, no comfortable bed in my own room, surrounded by signs of living.

Mobius must have known this. They have my file, just as they have everyone else's.

I finish the puzzle. The screen chirps as the artwork disappears, replaced by a complicated calculus equation. If I turn quickly enough from the screen and towards the sleek, dark dome of the Pod's shell wall beside my head, I can catch a glimpse of my reflection.

I look like shit.

It's hardly surprising, given the circumstances, but it's an unwelcome reminder nonetheless. As if it weren't enough that we've been stripped of our basic human rights, they had to rob us of our dignity as well.

It would've been all too easy to keep the Pods in perpetual darkness. There were many at the Pods' conception who thought it a waste of money to invest in "entertainment" for those sentenced. But the investors at Mobius Industries insisted that it was precisely that detail that would set us apart from other cities, like Toledryn, who still perform public executions like it's 2070 or something.

In all their campaigns, Mobius took care to explain that this is what made the Lazarus Accords so humane. To leave prisoners alone in a dark capsule with no mental stimulation would drive them mad. And society would have no use for such people upon their release.

But with engaging puzzles—something to occupy their minds and increase their intellectual capabilities—prisoners would remain sharp and be able to eventually rejoin society in a way that would benefit the masses.

Never the same puzzle twice— the Pods make sure of that. Mobius created them not just to provide a "revolutionary alternative to standard imprisonment," but to serve as learning computers, tracking which puzzles and equations take longer to solve and adjusting their metrics to increase the difficulty accordingly.

It takes me eight tries to correctly finish the equation before a brand new one takes its place.

There's a soft hiss to my right as a narrow slat opens up in the wall. I can't remember which meal this is, but I suppose it doesn't matter. I grab the energy bar and small block of ice just before the hatch snaps shut.

If I hold the bar right under my nose, I can smell granola, honey, and raisins. Artificial, of course—Mobius wouldn't waste the real thing on prisoners. They feed us the same meal every time, but it's the only thing I get to smell other than myself. I try to remember what other food smells like.

Warm, fluffy waffles, piled high with fresh fruit from the garden, dripping with pure maple syrup. Breakfast in bed after sleeping until noon.

Succulent chicken in truffle cream sauce. That one's Greta's specialty— none of our other chefs are worth what we pay them.

My stomach rumbles angrily.

Filet mignon. Filet mignon with porcini mushroom compound butter. Not the most modest of meals, but hell, I'd give my left arm for a good five courses right now.

I stuff the rest of the energy bar into my mouth and keep chipping away at the newest puzzle.

💾

"You're not hungry?"

I figured that after everything, he'd

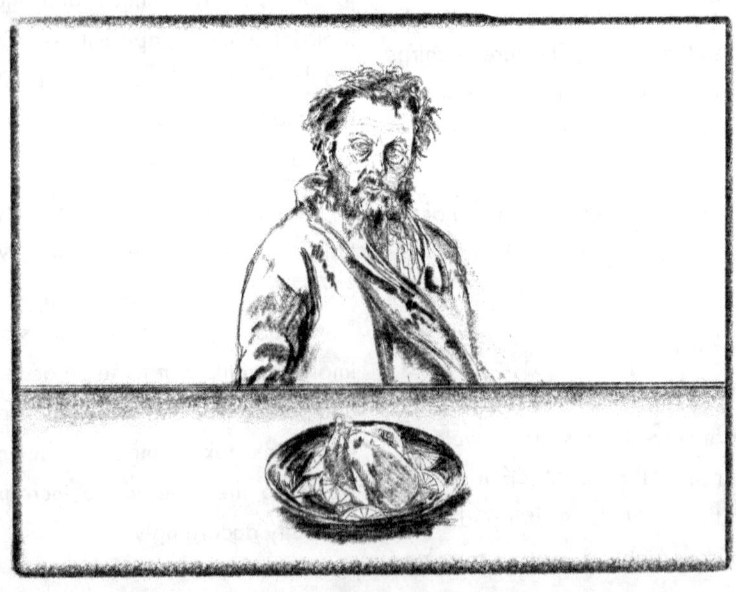

LAZARUS

be shoveling food into his mouth. I had to reserve this restaurant weeks in advance, taking the liberty of ordering the finest dishes on the menu—everything from lobster frittata to Cornish hens with garlic and rosemary.

They all sat untouched as Perseus Arnav simply stared at me from across the table.

"I'm just confused," he said, fiddling with the cuffs of his worn-out sleeve. "Why did you bring me here?"

There was no one next to us—I'd chosen this corner booth specifically—but I still cast a wary glance around the restaurant. "We need your help."

"We?"

"Me, my sister, several others who joined the cause. A voice like yours would really amplify our effect on the public."

Said voice wavered when it spoke next. "A-and I can appreciate that, it's just...."

He was hunched over, his eyes wide as if he'd just been spooked, his face prematurely lined. I remembered with perfect clarity when I'd first seen him weeks ago. His release had been on every network—non-stop footage of a delicate, sickly man, a shadow of who he once was, barely able to meet the public's eye as he was escorted to Mobius' headquarters. His eyes were dark with the weight of his trauma—radiating an aura of raw honesty that was truly captivating.

"They can't keep getting away with this," I said, gesturing outside.

The Lazarus Pods glided on their circular track far above the city. It was disgraceful. It was expected that the Pods should be visible from the lower districts, but certainly not from here.

"People are imprisoned every day, and those who aren't deemed useful after their release are disposed of, like they're nothing. People need to know the truth."

Perseus shook his head. "I'd rather just go back to my life—try to get things back to normal and put that whole experience out of my mind."

"But if we had a first-hand account, we could really show people how degrading the Lazarus Pods are. Mobius will have no choice but to abandon their project or face a public revolt." I reached into my suit jacket. "Please, reconsider the offer. I'll take care of everything."

His eyes widened as I slid the check across the table. "Mr. D'Avignon, I can't take your mon—"

"You know my family name, so you know money is of no consequence."

"It's not that." He studied me carefully, trying to figure me out. Finally, he sighed. "You're just a kid."

"I'm more than that." Causes like this were nothing new. Activism was a never-ending job—one that I've been able to perform to great effect. "Think of it as support. From a friend—an ally—who wants to help."

Perseus stared at the check for a long time. Then he glanced back up at me, a cautious smile pulling at his lips. "I'll do what I can."

We shook on it.

💾

I take a moment to relish the cracking of my knuckles as I break from the rapid-fire visual memory game that's been blinking at me for some time now. The implant in my lower abdomen pricks, the pain gone as fast as it came.

Intravenous waste elimination. Mobius Industries really thought of everything, didn't they. Can't have their prisoners soiling themselves in tiny compartments, not when someone would eventually have to clean the mess at the prisoner's release. Wouldn't want people to talk about how inhumane their prison conditions are.

I'm trying to take my time on the memory game, because even though I've been staring at nearly identical colored tiles for what feels like hours, it's still preferable to calculus.

I never excelled at math. Though to be fair, I didn't excel in any of my studies. The Academy spent far too long teaching subjects of no consequence, favoring academic busywork over addressing the real issues. Fey never minded, finding that she quite enjoyed our lectures in math, science, or engineering.

But I knew that true education must take place outside the lecture halls—why should we waste our time in a classroom when there was injustice and inequality on the streets? When there were people in need of help?

Someone had to step up—someone had to speak on behalf of those less fortunate.

And that might as well be me.

💾

"What are you talking about?"

Perseus steeled his jaw before repeating himself. "I can't do this anymore. I'm exhausted, Dante, it—it's too much."

I pulled him aside, away from the crowd that had gathered, rumbling in response to our speech. "But we're making progress, we're getting the message out there."

We'd been making the news every night as they followed our growing resistance. "Think of all the districts we've been able to visit in the last few months alone! The hotels, the gourmet meals... The people love us, they support what we're doing. We couldn't have made it this far without you."

He looked unconvinced, still as thin and pale as ever. "You don't understand. It's barely been a year since—"

"We needed a fresh perspective," I explained, hoping my voice would calm him, drown out the battle cries behind us. "Mobius can't ignore publicity like this for much longer without making a statement. If we gain enough traction, if enough people join the protest, we can shut them down for good, stop them from ever—"

"And I'm telling you I can't keep doing this!" Perseus raised his voice in a way I'd never heard before. It broke on the last word. "I can't keep reliving it— ten years in a cell the size of a casket, and..." His breath came faster, and he struggled to keep speaking. "I don't feel right, I-I can't...."

I stepped closer, moving slowly as Perseus tensed. When it was clear he wouldn't run or push me away, I touched his shoulder. "You overcame the greatest hell imaginable and lived to tell the tale. Not many others are as well-adjusted after their release."

Perseus sniffed, and I realized that he was fighting tears. He rubbed his eyes. "I just—" he gasped, and I had to lean closer to hear, "I don't feel strong enough."

A single tear slid down his ragged cheek, the very picture of a brave young veteran, heroically facing the world that broke him. The tear was a great touch—no one with a conscience would be able to resist that kind of open vulnerability. I wondered if we could get it on camera next time.

"You are," I assured him. "The rallies are working. We're blowing up the networks, and Mobius knows they can't stop what we've begun here. Word on the street, the photo ops, our talking points in each of the districts—the momentum is only going to grow. You just need to have faith in our message. We can do it. Together."

🖫

What I wouldn't give to sit up, take a shit. I do my best to crack the joints in my back and neck. Mobius has robbed me of one of life's simplest pleasures— for that alone, they deserve to burn.

How long will it take my eyes

to re-adjust to the sunlight, or even anything other than the artificial glow of a touchscreen? How long until the muscles in my legs remember how to run?

How long until I'm able to mark the passage of time with something other than the number of puzzles completed and energy bars consumed?

I think of home—of the maze in the garden where Fey and I would get lost as kids, of the studio in our east wing where she would study her engineering blueprints while I crafted my latest campaign.

It didn't take much to convince Fey to partake, to lend her practical knowledge and analytical approaches to the mission that we both now pursued. We were an unstoppable team—she, the logical, pragmatic strategist, and me, the fire and motivation needed to get it done.

I heard it on the news like everyone else.

Fey called me into the parlor, her face white as she pulled up the screen. We both froze as the images played out across our wall.

I couldn't make it out at first. The filming was erratic as the camera crew and reporters bottle-necked their way inside a homely little place somewhere in the lower districts. Voices overlapped as we were brought inside the house, the camera lingering with sudden focus on the body that lay slumped in a dirty bathtub.

Even as I stared at Perseus Arnav's face, I couldn't believe it was him.

The reporters kept talking, but their voices sounded garbled through the thick fog that settled around me. Something about blood on his wrists... no family, no next of kin....

It didn't make sense.

"I don't understand," Fey whispered, speaking past the hand over her mouth.

Words of disbelief and horror choked me. It felt like I didn't have any words at all in the weeks that followed, up until I sat in a courtroom facing a jury consisting entirely of executives from Mobius Industries.

The prosecutor glared at me from across the box where I sat. "In the case involving the death of Perseus Arnav, how do you plead?"

"Not guilty," I insisted, for what felt like the hundredth time. "I had nothing to do with it!"

The prosecutor's eyes glinted and narrowed as he swept across the room, heels clicking rhythmically over the black marble floor. He swiped the screen on his Mobi-Tech watch to project images of Perseus and I into a hologram in the center of the room.

"Mr. D'Avignon, there is substantial evidence, from eyewitnesses as well as various recordings, of the two of you being well acquainted, working together to incite the riots that have been plaguing our city for months now."

"You're really accusing me of murder?" I countered, incredulously. I gestured to Fey, who sat on the side of the defense, still shaking in anger from her testimony. "My sister already attested that we were both at home at the time, just us and our staff."

"Do you know what I think, Mr. D'Avignon?" The prosecutor moved closer, his leering face tinted blue in the light of the hologram playing silently behind him. "I think you were the mastermind behind these uprisings. I think you took advantage of a vulnerable ex-detainee, exploited him for your own gain, forced him to relive his trauma, and bullied him into committing suicide, what do you think about that?"

"I think that's ridiculous and this entire trial is a farce," I snapped, meeting the eye of each of the jurors. "I've already been proven innocent in this man's death, which is what this trial is supposed to be about."

They didn't bother with closing statements. The jury ruled unanimously in favor of conviction, and the judge passed sentence within minutes.

Five years. Five years, with no way of knowing how much is left.

My knuckles crack against the ceiling as I punch it, succeeding only in breaking the skin and sending a shooting pain through my arm.

Over and over, Perseus' face sneaks behind my eyelids, his dark eyes glazed as they'd lifted him onto the stretcher.

I'd seen him just days before, at our most recent press conference. He'd spoken quietly, as ever, his whole persona soft and raw as he spoke about his imprisonment. It was the same routine as always—he hadn't even had an outburst since the one time he'd lost faith in our mission.

The prosecutor's smug accusations seem to echo through the Pod. *Took advantage, exploited, bullied...*

No, that was slander. I would never bully anyone, and no one could say that I treated Perseus with anything less than the utmost respect. No one understood him like I did. He just needed someone to listen, to help tell his story.

Perseus' voice, louder in my head than it had ever been in life: "I don't feel strong enough."

He'd been so small in that moment, something unhinged in his eyes as he'd pleaded with me. Had he been planning his fate since that day? Was that conversation—one of the last we'd had—the final straw?

Maybe he was as broken as he'd said.

Maybe I should have done more to help him.

But...he was strong. Perseus Arnav was a fighter, stronger and braver than anyone I'd ever known.

Mobius did this to him. That's what corporate assholes do, what they've always done.

They wanted me out of the way. I was leading a vocal protest that was gaining momentum, and they needed me out of the way. And this was the perfect way to do it.

Mobius Industries will pay. If it takes another five years, or a hundred more rallies, they will pay for what they did to him.

What they did to us.

The screen chirps, and I set to work on the next puzzle.

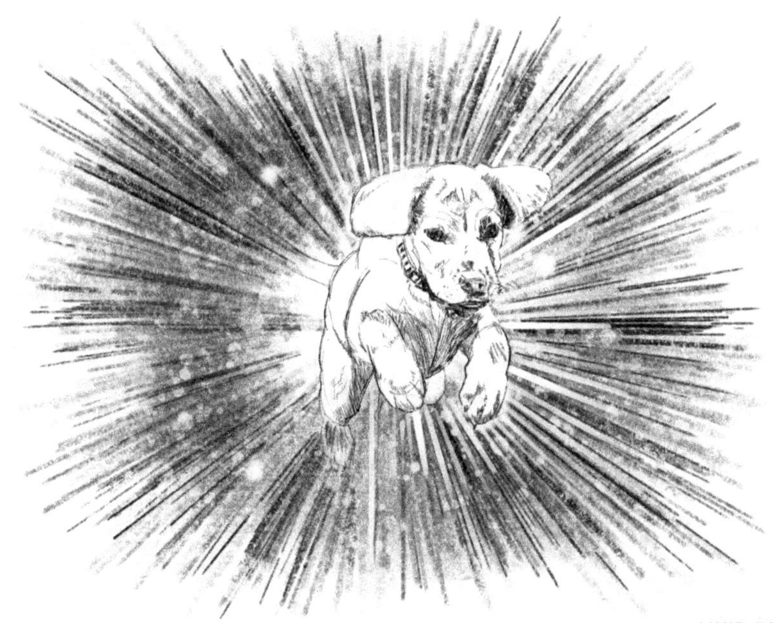

LUKE FOSTER

GOOD BOY

Brad and Melanie heard thumping from baby Jack's room, and knew he wasn't just jumping in his crib.

Brad pushed open the door, afraid his son had fallen out and hurt himself. With a sigh of relief, he saw that the baby was safe in his crib.

"Hey, big guy," Brad said to his son as he entered the room. "What's all the noise in—"

"Brad!" Melanie shouted as she looked past her husband.

A growling, full-grown, yellow Labrador was standing in the corner of the room. It had something in its mouth.

How this strange dog had gotten into their son's room, and whatever it was holding, they didn't care. The only thing on their minds was keeping their son safe.

Not that Jack seemed to mind the intruder. Quite the opposite, in fact.

"Puh! Puh! Puh!" he yelled in delight, pointing at the dog.

Brad raised one arm to shield his son should the animal leap at him.

"Stay in your crib, sport."

The light was still off, but Melanie didn't want to risk taking her eyes off the dog to flip the switch. Instead, she picked up a toy chair. It was light plastic, but the closest thing the room had to a weapon. She walked slowly towards the dog, ready to swing if the animal attacked.

The dog dropped the thing in its mouth and ran by them. Melanie swung the chair and missed. Brad shouted and kicked at the creature, also missing. The dog ran down the hallway and into the bathroom.

Melanie sprang after it, and seconds later Brad heard her yell. He spared a glance at Jack—still safe in his crib—before running after his wife.

Melanie stood in the bathroom, the chair dangling in one hand. The light was on. The window—shut. The bathroom—empty.

"Where'd it go?" Brad asked.

"I... I don't know."

"Downstairs?"

"It couldn't have," Melanie said in a small voice. "I watched it run in here. I was right behind it."

"Well, it couldn't have just disappeared!"

"I know that, Brad, but...."

"Puh!"

Brad and Melanie ran back to their son. Brad flipped on the light and exhaled. The dog hadn't come back. Jack looked at his parents in confusion.

"Puh?"

Melanie picked her son out of his crib and hugged him tight.

"It's okay, baby. Mommy and daddy are here now. The mean dog is gone and he's not gonna hurt y—"

"Melanie."

There was no fear in Brad's voice, just an eerie calm. Melanie turned and saw Brad pointing to where the dog had been when they first entered. She followed his gaze and gasped. She saw what the dog had been holding in its mouth.

A dead rat.

Melanie shielded Jack's eyes and turned away herself.

"Oh, God, Brad, is it..."

Brad knelt cautiously in front of the rat. Its teeth were covered in flecks of blood and an ugly-looking foam was coming from its mouth. Brad was no expert, but he suspected the rat had rabies.

"Yeah, it's dead. It's got a lot of bite marks in it. The dog killed it."

Brad stood and looked at Melanie.

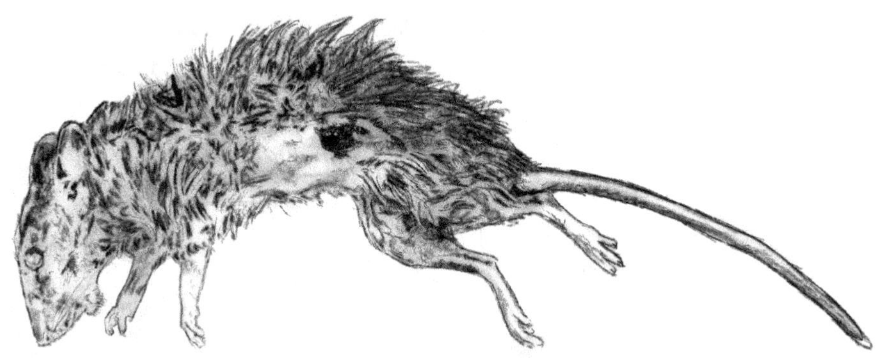

Jack burbled away in his mother's arms, not a care in the world.

"Melanie," Brad said. "What just happened?"

💾 9 💾

JJ ran as fast as he could. It wasn't going to be fast enough.

Big Mike and Pete were after him. They had been threatening him for weeks. They told him a beating was coming if he didn't do their homework. JJ was smart and small and too afraid to stand up for himself. So he did their homework every day, until yesterday, when his mom picked him up early from school and he didn't have time to get their assignments. Now they were following through on their threats. If only they were as lazy chasing him as they were with their math.

JJ huffed as he ran for the woods. He spent a lot of time by himself there, and knew the terrain like the back of his hand. If he could just get to the woods he'd be safe. If he could—

JJ lurched back with a strangled squawk as Pete grabbed his shirt collar. JJ hit the ground hard.

"I told ya not to make us run, ya little bastard," Pete said as he stared down at JJ. "Now you're gonna pay."

Big Mike slugged JJ in the stomach. JJ doubled over, air rushing out of his lungs. Tears filled his eyes.

"What's the matter, nerd?" Pete asked. "Ya gonna cry for mommy?"

JJ gasped for breath as he prepared to be hit again. But he wasn't.

JJ heard Big Mike yell something. He saw the bully thrashing around, but couldn't tell why through his tears. He wiped his eyes and saw a dog clinging to Big Mike's arm. It was bigger than a puppy, but not fully grown. It was yellow, but JJ wasn't sure what kind it was. His parents wouldn't let him have one.

Big Mike spun around, howling and swearing as blood poured from the dog's maw. It had the boy's arm in a death grip, and it wasn't letting go for all the bones at the pet store. Pete swatted at the dog, but it wouldn't let go. Big Mike's bravado fell, and he started to cry.

The dog finally released its grip and dropped to the ground. Big Mike collapsed, holding his bleeding arm, tears and snot running down his face. JJ couldn't help it. Despite his fear and confusion, he let out a giggle.

The dog, meanwhile, planted itself between JJ and Pete, and growled at the larger boy. Pete had one secret he never shared with anyone, not even Big Mike: he was scared of dogs. Terrified, in fact. But right now, watching the dog bare its teeth and watching Big Mike's blood dripping off the animal's fangs, all thoughts of bravery were abandoned. He ran away screaming.

The dog turned to Big Mike and took one step closer. Big Mike stood up, stumbled, stood up again, and took off, cradling his bloody arm.

"Yeah! You wussies better run!" JJ yelled at his tormentors' backs. As soon as they were out of sight, JJ collapsed. The whole ordeal had felt like hours, but it couldn't have been more than a minute or two. He couldn't believe how lucky he'd gotten. If that dog hadn't shown up when it did...

JJ looked up. The dog was still there. All the viciousness had gone out of its eyes and it stared at JJ with a mix of curiosity and concern.

"Hey, pal," JJ said. "Thanks for saving me. Good dog."

JJ slowly reached out his hand. The dog walked over and put his head under his hand, moving it around so JJ couldn't help but pet him. JJ laughed, this time with relief and happiness instead of nervous tension.

"What's your name, boy? Where are you from?" JJ searched for a collar and tag. Nothing. The dog could be a stray as far as he knew.

"You hungry, boy? You want to come home with me?"

The dog perked up when JJ said "home." It sniffed at the boy's hand and face. Abruptly, it pulled back. He barked once, then turned and ran for the woods.

JJ followed. "Hey, boy! Come on! Where are you going?"

He ran into the woods and looked around. There was no sign of the dog.

"You there, boy? C'mere!"

JJ whistled and slapped his

hand against his thigh, but the dog never showed.

JJ searched the woods for two hours. The dog was gone.

💾 **16** 💾

Johnny didn't want to cry. Crying was for kids. He wasn't going to cry, dammit. He *wasn't*.

Johnny looked at his phone. The text message hadn't changed in the last three hours, no matter how much he wanted it to.

A single drop of salty water splashed on the screen, partially obscuring Kelly's message. Johnny wiped his eyes. Dammit. Derek. Of course it was Derek.

Johnny never liked Derek. He knew Kelly thought he was cute. But she told him not to be jealous. *Johnny* was her boyfriend.

But, apparently, so was Derek. He had been for a month. And she couldn't even tell him in person. She had to send a damn text.

Johnny couldn't hold the tears back. Or the sobs. He dropped his phone and started bawling. He finally thought he had done it. He finally thought he had found someone. He didn't just have a friend, he had a *girlfriend*. But now it was worse than just being alone. Now he was alone *and* a laughingstock. He could only imagine what her friends were saying about him. What *Derek's* friends were saying about him. The awkward science dork who thought he was in the same league as Kelly Kirkp—

"Guh!" Johnny yelped through his sobs. Something had bumped his foot. He looked down. It was a puppy.

Where did a puppy come from? This wide-open stretch of land had been his and Kelly's spot. He loved taking her here and showing her the stars and explaining the physics of how the universe worked. At the time she seemed interested. No one ever came here—they certainly didn't walk their dogs here—and he would have heard an animal walking through the dry grass. But there it was, wagging his tail and staring up at him with its bright, brown eyes.

"Hey, boy," Johnny said through his tears. "Where's your owner?"

Johnny wiped his eyes and tried to compose himself. He didn't want anyone to see him crying. But no owner showed. Johnny lowered his hands to see if the dog would let him pick it up. He shouldn't have worried. The dog jumped right into his arms. The force knocked Johnny back a little, and he couldn't help but smile.

"Whoa, boy! Easy!" Johnny said.

The puppy yelped and started licking Johnny's face. Johnny laughed. He couldn't remember the last time he had done that. Johnny held the puppy to his chest, for how long he didn't know. He just let the dog lick his hands and his chin and felt loved in the way a teenage boy with a broken heart never thought he could feel again.

Johnny watched as the puppy fell asleep in his arms. The little guy probably didn't have a home. Well, he could fix that. His parents wouldn't mind, he was sure of it. He stood up and was about to start walking home when he remembered his phone. He put the sleeping dog down, turned around, and picked up the phone. He turned back around.

"Okay, buddy. Time to—"

The dog was gone.

Johnny looked around. The dog hadn't run off. It was just...gone. Johnny walked around for a bit, certain the puppy had woken up and ran off to play, but he couldn't find it anywhere.

Johnny stopped. The dog *had* been there, right? It wasn't just a dream?

No, no, he was sure it had been there. Where it had gone, though, was anyone's guess.

Johnny wasn't sure he could take losing two loves in one day, but he was surprised to find he didn't feel as terrible as he did even an hour ago. He was still sad, sure, and he would be sad for a while, but he was going to be okay.

He was going to be okay.

💾 31 💾

"Dude, seriously, you brought your *dog* in here?"

Dr. Stashford stared at Dr. Plemons in disbelief. As smart as Plemons was, he made some boneheaded decisions sometimes.

"I couldn't help it, Stash," Plemons replied. "I was walking him and I finally figured out what was going wrong with the chrono generator."

Stash looked past Plemons and at the puppy, its leash tied to a chair, and his heart softened. Plemons had been despondent since Suzie died, and the little Labrador had pulled him out of a worryingly dark place.

"All right, man, but he stays in the observation room."

"Of course."

Stash looked at him impatiently. "So, the generator?"

"Yes, yes," Plemons said as the two stepped into the laboratory. "We've been looking at the calculations all wrong."

Plemons stopped in front of a computer hooked up to the generator. His fingers danced over the keyboard as he typed a series of equations into the machine. "If we want to create the proper tachyon bursts, we need to compensate for the negative numbers like this and...like so, and..."

"You gonna tell me what you're doing?" Stash asked.

"Almost...there!" Plemons said, not hearing Stash. Plemons grabbed Stash's arm. "Come on, let's test it out!"

The two stepped into the control room. Plemons turned on the generator. It started to hum.

"Aw, yes," Stash said. "Sounds like we got some time energy!"

Plemons nodded in agreement. The machine hummed louder. The generator was working. The field was growing as it should and—

A burst of energy shot from the generator and slapped into the wall, leaving a brownish-black mark in its wake. It stank of age and decay rather than a burning smell.

"Whoa!" Stash said. "That ain't good!"

"Not good at all," Plemons said. He looked worryingly down at the controls. "Something's gone wrong with..."

Whatever he was going to say next, Plemons never said it, because another bolt of energy blasted from the machine and hit the wall, leaving another aging mark in its wake.

"No no no no no!" Plemons shouted, running his hands through his hair. "The whole thing's going to overheat!"

"I can't shut it down!" Stash shouted. "We've lost all control from this end!"

Plemons yanked the door open. Stash grabbed his arm before he could leave the room. "What the hell do you think you're doing?"

"If we don't shut that machine down, everyone in this building could be killed!"

Plemons shoved Stash back and ran out to the machine. Stash watched helplessly as his friend tapped frantically at the controls. He wanted to help, but of course Plemons hadn't shared his calculations.

Movement out of the corner of Stash's eye caught his attention. Plemons' dog had somehow freed himself from his collar and was barking frantically at the window of the observation room. A stray beam from the generator arced its way in that direction. Stash wasn't sure if it hit the dog or not, but it sure looked like it did.

Stash looked back at Plemons and

the generator. It seemed like his friend was starting to get things under control. Plemons seemed to think so, too.

"I've got it, Stash!" He shouted triumphantly. "I've got..."

But the machine wasn't going down quietly. A final burst of energy expanded outward from the generator. Plemons barely had time to register the shock before he was consumed.

"Plemons!" Stash screamed. "Johhhhn!"

Stash could barely move. He could hardly register what had just happened. Plemons was gone. All that was left were two noises: the quiet, angry hum of the chrono machine as it crackled with its remaining energy, and a loud sound from the observation room. The door pushed open and Stash realized the sound was Plemons' dog, barking in anger and fear for its master.

"Get out of there!" Stash yelled, snapping back to the moment. "It's not safe!"

Stash pulled the control room door open and ran out as the puppy bounded toward the generator. It sniffed at the ground where Plemons had stood less than a minute before, barked, and, in a moment Stash would remember until the day he died, disappeared in a flash of light.

💾 *Everywhen* 💾

Even though he had only been alive for a few months, what the puppy saw was unlike anything he had ever seen before. He had no scope for explaining what was all around him. It was John-master, many John-masters, but wrong ones. They looked wrong. They looked like John-master, but John-master as if he were one of the small people they saw at the park. But maybe they knew how to find the right John-master. He moved towards one.

This one was crying in a field and saying a name the puppy didn't recognize. He nudged this John-master until he picked him up. Then the dog licked his face until this wrong John-master felt better and the pup dozed off. He quickly woke up and knew he couldn't stay. He had to find the right John-master.

He moved on. An older John-master was sitting on a bench reading a big book. He let John-master pet him and he moved on.

He saved a wrong John-master from an attack by bigger boys. He watched from a window as the woman John-master called Suzie stopped moving. He found a younger John-master and tripped him so he'd fall in front of a young Suzie-master. John-master blushed. Suzie-master smiled. And he moved on.

Sometimes he'd stay for weeks, watching John-master from a distance, trying to learn if he was the right one. Sometimes he'd only stay for a few minutes. Sometimes he'd play with the young John-master. Sometimes he'd kill an animal that threatened the puppy version of John-master. But it would always be the wrong John-master. So he would move on. And on. And on.

And on.

💾 82 💾

John sat alone, leaning against a stone and looking at the stars. His rebreather hummed as he inhaled and whistled as he exhaled. He was so very tired.

The last five decades has been long ones. John had been used to loneliness over his long life, but the first three decades paled in comparison to what happened after the accident. This time period was as foreign to him as his era would have been to the dinosaurs. Earth was long gone, the human race gone even longer.

He had met other peoples of course. So many people here at the quiet end of the universe. But if he was alone among his own kind, he was even more isolated when surrounded by species made of

song and cultures that communicated with a language of smell.

So he came here, to this little rock in space. He built a house that took care of him. It served all his needs so he could spend his time trying to get back to where he belonged. But the science that caused the accident was an anomaly. He was never able to recreate what happened that fateful day.

So he sat and waited. Waited for what would have to happen eventually. Day after day, he waited.

But today, something unusual happened. He heard a shuffling noise and turned. It was a dog. A Labrador. Probably a yellow lab, but his hair had long since turned white. He walked with a shuffle, arthritis seizing up his joints. His eyes were cloudy, the same as any man's would be if they lived as long as the dog.

"Hey, boy," John said with no surprise in his voice. "It's been a while. I wondered when you'd show up."

The dog shuffled over to John. He sniffed the man, then rubbed his muzzle against the old man's face. He looked wrong, but he knew it was his John-master. Finally.

"I knew you'd come, pal. My whole life, you were always there when I needed you most."

The dog lay his head down on the man's lap. He had walked so much and was so very tired.

John looked down at the dog. He was tired too, but not too tired to show his friend love. He slowly pet the dog's head.

"You just rest, pal. You're home now."

The dog closed his eyes. He knew he was home, too.

John leaned back and looked up. The stars were getting dimmer. Or was it his eyes? He didn't know. Nor did he care.

"You can sleep now, pal," John said, stroking fur he hadn't touched in five decades. He kept petting as he closed his eyes.

"Good boy."

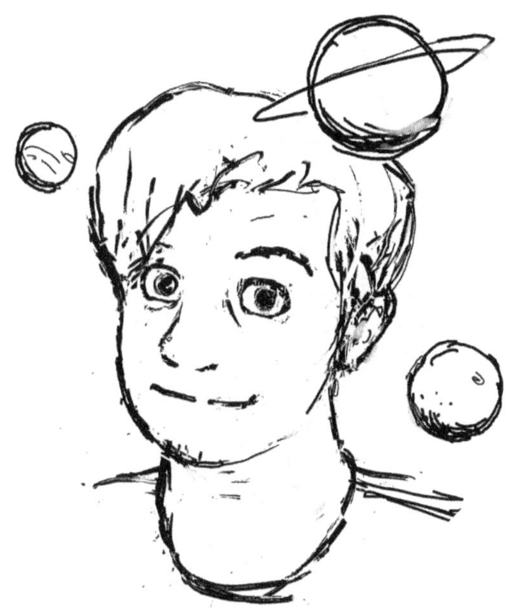

COVER ART: JORDAN ALARCON

Born in the supple, meaty womb of Southern California, Jordan is an aspiring Wunderkind and storyboard artist. He spends his time listening to German opera, befriending all the dogs, and making butt jokes. He likes pine trees, the color yellow, and talking about—but not listening to—smooth jazz. He spends his days creating mad-lib templates to supercharge his artist bio writing process.

Jordan's work can be found on Instagram at @jordanalarcon.

PLANET SCUMM: What is your favorite animal and why?

JORDAN ALARCON: I love the American Bison the most because of how sturdy they are. They're big, they're free, they run towards the storm, which I think is a powerful image.

They're nature's rectangle and I relate to that.

PS: What was the inspiration behind your *Planet Scumm* artwork?

JA: A lot of this painting was influenced by the work of Italian futurist artist,

Luigi Russolo—specifically his use of concentric circles.

Obviously, the story that it's based on, *Bookends* was a huge inspiration too. I really found it charming and engaging.

The pose of the figure in front is partially a nod to Nirvana's *Nevermind*. I don't know how that links up thematically, but it came to mind when I was designing.

PS: What did you learn while making this piece?

JA: I learned a lot about my own workflow. In the past, with projects like this, I tended to kind of make it up as I went along. This was the first time that I really made an effort to know exactly what I was doing before I got started. I wrote everything down in a text file that had all the design elements I wanted to include, all the color choices and how it related to the story.

From there I made a bunch of thumbnails and picked the best one. Even after all that prep, I still had all sorts of great little spontaneous moments that made it into the final cover, which I think I was afraid wouldn't get if I planned so much. I'll be taking all of that with me moving forward.

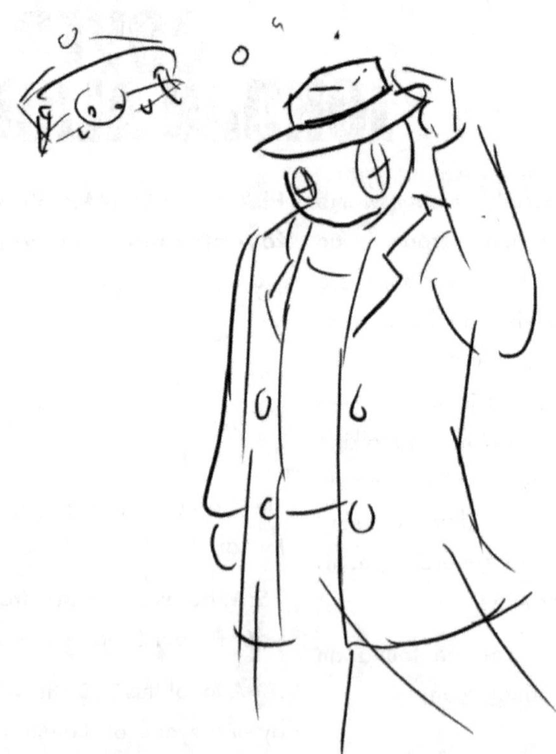

    COVER ART: JORDAN ALARCON

PS: Marry/smooch/kill: The works of Nietzche, Lord Byron, and Kanye West.

JA: Smooch Lord Byron, cause he's the original bad-boy of poetry, marry Nietzche, because his mix of nihilism and self improvement speaks to me, and kill Kanye West, not because I want to, but because the format of the question dictates that I do.

PS: If the robots take over and impose a system of fascism that in practice works better than our democratic govt would you rebel or conform?

JA: That depends, I guess. Like, are they racist robots? I can't really get down with that. If we're talking just about like, the cold unfeeling logic of robots vs the scrappy underdogginess of humans, I gotta say, I'm going with the robots.

Like, I've seen us as a species in action, and I'm pretty sure that what humanity needs is some outside force to take our keys away and tuck us into bed, y'know? If robots can be that for us, I'm on board. I'd rather they didn't kill us though. Or use us for fuel or whatever.

PS: What are you working on now?

JA: Right now I'm in school, training to be a storyboard artist.

I'm also working on an art book about a deep-sea-diver who's also a noir-detective. [Concept sketch to the left.] Other than that I'm just trying to wrap my hands around social media.

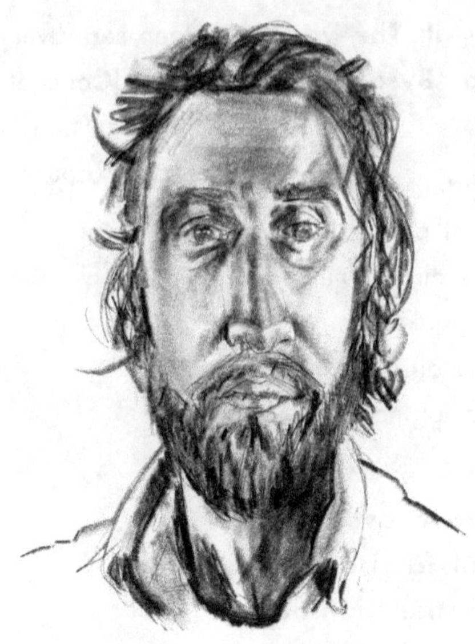

SPOT ILLUSTRATIONS: SAM RHEAUME

Sam grew up as a small puppy that met a magical pond toad that granted him three wishes. He wasted the first two on frivolous things like sidewalk chalk and Brie until he wisened up and used the last to turn into a human because humans can go on walks whenever they want. He's been making art ever since.

Sam is currently travelling the world and living that digital nomad life. More of his work can be found on social media at @sirheaume or at samrheaume.com.

PLANET SCUMM: What is your favorite animal and why?

SAM RHEAUME: Penguins because of their tenacity. They tried to move into Europe and the Chimeras and Dragons were like 'nah.' Then they tried to move to America and the elk and moose were like 'you're funny looking.' And then they tried to move to Australia and the kangaroos were like 'you're a bit smelly, m8.' And then they tried to move to South America and the Capibara were like 'nah we've got it covered.' And then they tried to move to Africa and the elephants were like 'yeah maybe, I just have to ask my mom' and then never got back to the poor penguins. Finally they tried to move to Asia and the Panda bears just stared blankly at the penguins without response.

So finally the penguins were like 'Fuck it. And fuck you all. I don't care if Antarctica is the coldest place on earth, we're going to live there and have dope ragers and gorge ourselves on krill.' And so they party until the sun goes down. And sometimes in Antarctica the sun never goes down.

That's what Penguins are all about.

PS: What was the inspiration behind your *Planet Scumm* artwork?

SR: Old galaxy mag spots! I wanted to take a more tonal, traditional media approach to the illustrations. Add some depth and detail compared to the cartoony style of past illustrations.

PS: What did you learn while making this piece?

SR: I'm getting better at drawing machines and devices. I'm a figurative draughtsman and love drawing people. Machines come less naturally to me, but I am enjoying getting better.

PS: Marry/smooch/kill: The works of Nietzche, Lord Byron, and Kanye West.

SR: These are famously unstable individuals to be forcing me to relate to in such intimate ways as betrothal and murder. But if it's their ouvres I am relating to...

Byron get's drowned in the English Channel because who cares?

Kanye gets smooched because I am convinced he's like those magic eye pictures: too close or two far it's just noise, but if you look just right with your eyes crossed you see a unicorn.

I marry Nietchze because that's the kind of sad fuck I am. At least the marriage is constantly evolving, swining between states of exhaltation and deterioration.

PS: If the robots take over and impose a system of fascism that in practice works better than our democratic govt would you rebel or conform?

SR: This question brings me back to 2010 when I was reading Camus' "The Rebel" and feeling like a fueled-up 20-year-old revolutionary. It would be all about how the robots process and implement justice.

The deliberation boils down to a couple of key questions: "Would a supremely rational system of government aleviate unfairness in passing judgement?" and "Is human phenomenology a monolith or will there always be enough disparity between tribes and individuals that perceived unfairness is inevitable?"

With these questions in mind, my guess is that rebellion would break out, but it wouldn't necessarily be people vs. robots. More likely it would be rebels vs. an elite whose positions the robots have deemed as higher or more just. For as egalatarian as a robot society might be, as governors of humans passing such judgement would be inevitable. At the end of the day it almost always ends up being people vs. people, unfortunately.

My role? Embedded photo journalist with the rebels.

PS: What are you working on now?

SR: I have some actual design clients! So right now I am still working on a few labels and illustrations. I recently finished a logo for a tincture line for a friend.

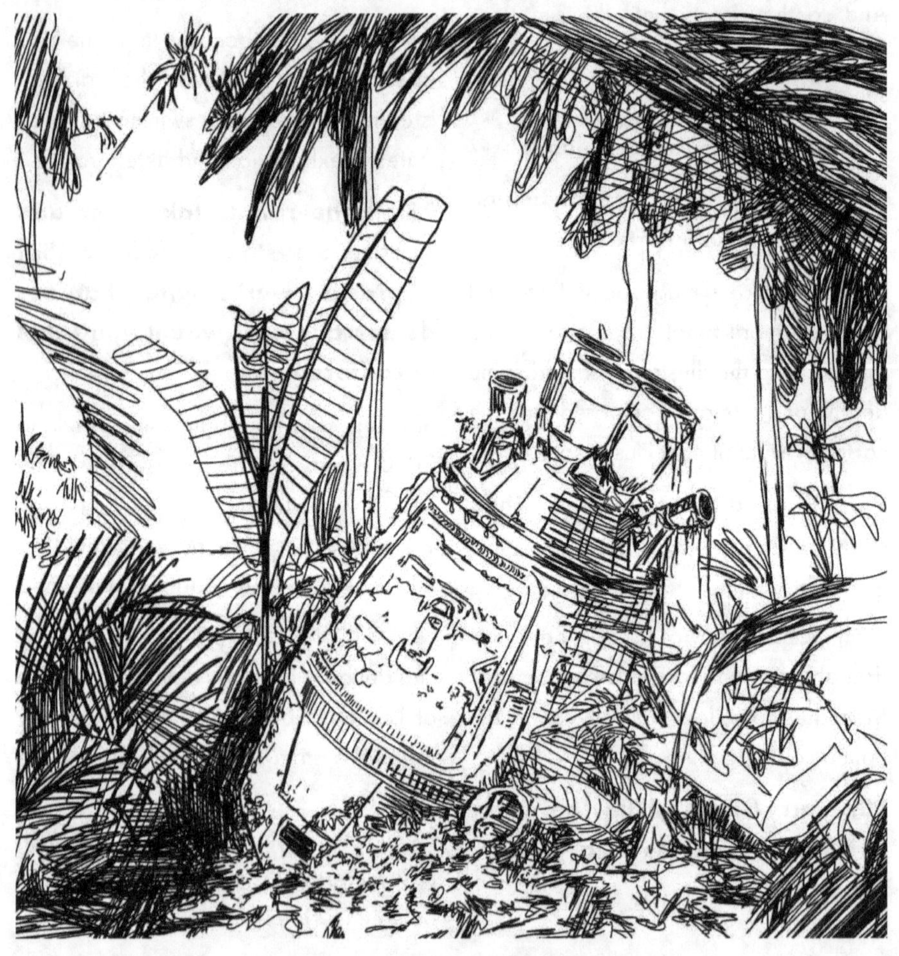

SPOT ILLUSTRATIONS: SAM RHEAUME